FORTY-SEVEN SECONDS
Business Edition

FORTY-SEVEN SECONDS

Business Edition

By

Mark Williams

Special Agent (Ret)

Dedication

To the sheep dogs. For their loyalty

to perfect, sacrificial love.

And to the common man or woman,

whose noble heart and common sense

always wins the day.

Special thanks

to the editing and advisory team:

Front and back cover design, page design and text editing by Bob Ryan,
Bob Ryan Writing Creative | Phoenix, Arizona

Back Cover author photo: Lori Wooldridge International Ltd.,
San Francisco, London, Bishop's-Stortford

Forty-Seven Seconds, Business Edition

Copyright © 2022 Mark Williams. All rights reserved.

*No part of this book may be reproduced or transmitted in any form
or by any means without the written permission of the author.*
www.fortysevensecondsusa.com

Forty-Seven Seconds

Mark Williams

About This Book...

Forty-Seven Seconds, Business Edition has hit the target in safety training! It would be a great read for every medium to large business in this country. For that matter, it would be a great read for anyone who supervises employees in and is responsible for the safety of the business site! Safety workshops should be designed and taught based on the wealth of information found in this book.
—Matthew Young, Bank Executive

Forty-Seven Seconds, Business Edition is an outstanding resource of useful information for educators and supervisors, which provides a common sense approach to what to do and how to prepare for a variety of unthinkable safety situations. The information found in *Forty-Seven Seconds* can lead to the survival of such events.
—Nancy L. Kloss, administrator

A superb resource for the workplace. Every year, hundreds now are killed by violence in our workplace, houses of worship, or social gathering places. The book is a lifesaving, life changing resource, an effective and vital tool to help us to make our part of the world a safer place.
—Lt. Col. Dave Grossman
Author of On Killing, On Combat, and Assassination Generation

Speaking as a retired U.S. Army Major, former Sheriff's Detective ***Forty-Seven Seconds, Business Edition is not a fluff manual with dream solutions,*** but the perfect tool. It's not only for educators, but for the Whole community—businesses, churches, hospitals—to help protect themselves, reduce liability, and take control of situations they might find themselves in, in an ever-changing world.
—Billy A. Gumm Det. Ret.

Forty-Seven Seconds

I am in a violent combat arena
that just a few minutes ago was a calm school or work place.
Now, I am fighting for my life.

I could hide, fight, flee, posture, or submit.
Whatever gets me to the end of the day and to my family alive
is what I will use to get there.

How about you?

Mark Williams

Table of Contents

Introduction 4

The Lockdown 11

Shelter in Place 21

The Evacuation 27

The Boogeyman 39

The Cavalry 48

Get Small, Get Quiet 54

What Wil I Do To Survive? 65

Weather Events 71

Postscript 77

Tear-out Sheet 79

Forty-Seven Seconds

Mark Williams

Author's Foreword

When I was in law enforcement, training was the key to life. It was also absolutely some of the most boring time I've ever spent. It was boring because we did it over and over and over. You get what I'm saying. When my son went off for his two tours, I remember him commenting about that same issue—boredom. Doing the same thing, over and over, every time, doing the same thing. We both knew why. When you are in a high stress environment, your brain, the human computer, defaults to the data it knows, the data you loaded into it. You 'react' out of instinct rather than thought. You act. Muscles move because that is what they were trained to do. There is no time, there is no room to think. There is only action.

After I retired and then became a high school teacher, there was nothing but thinking. Terms like 'think-pair-share' or 'what I hear you say is…' filled my life, a different life—a good life. I had worked as a training instructor for years, sometimes in areas of safety and how to stay alive, and even think, in volatile situations. None of that existed in the educational world until 1999 when Columbine High School became a household term. September 11th took place just two years later and the country was having to wake up to a living nightmare.

Now, well, sometimes those events at schools or the workplace don't even make the lead story on the news. It is becoming, unfortunately, routine.

Stopping it requires a culture shift. That is not what is in these pages. What is here are clues and insights in to how to live for about twenty minutes. That's all. When the world around you becomes violent and that violence is preparing to land on you, either by another human, accident, or weather, what are you going to do? This book will start that thinking. It is short, easy to read and—I hope—engaging. It will provide a quick resource and tickle your common sense if I did my job right.

Enjoy.

Mark Williams

Forty-Seven Seconds

Mark Williams

Introduction

This book is titled Forty-Seven Seconds, Business Edition for two reasons. First, because that is the amount of time you have, as an employee, to secure your room, your space, your work area during extraordinary events like shootings. There are other things as well—like trying to understand those who want to hurt us or our co-workers, and maybe getting them help before they respond with violence. The second reason is because this is the Business Edition. The first edition was for schools and sure, you could use that one in the business arena, but you're reading this because you run, work, own, a business, and not a school. There are a few different concerns, not many, but significant enough for you people to own your own and share your concerns.

This book will discuss why we need to prepare for that moment when the news we see on TV becomes a reality in our own lives, and the scene is our own living room or work space. It's a nightmare most of us have never imagined themselves being in. I wrote this book because there is not one like it. Not one that talks about these things clearly, the way those in academia, or anywhere for that matter, really need to have them addressed.

As a former law enforcement instructor making the transition to education, I responded sometimes with a dumbfounded look at some of the safety issues I found in the educational arena.

It is pointed at you, Business Person. The days of school shootings being the lead story, well, they still should make the news, but businesses, churches, movie theaters, saloons, all are on the list now. The doctor's office you work in can also find help in its pages. You, walking down a mall and facing an unexpected and dangerous situation, may be able to tap into some of what you learn here if it ever becomes needed. Almost all of it is based on common sense, a term you will see used over and over and over again.

This is serious stuff, but I will try to deliver it with a lightness that is maybe a little easier to swallow. This is a deadly, worst-nightmare conversation and if we don't look at it with a little humor, well, it's just hard stuff. It's okay to laugh at some parts if you think they're funny. Some of the funniest times in my life were in situations that could have been news footage. I am sure some of you know what I am talking about. If we didn't see this in an open and easy way, I think it would make us all want to stay home, lock the doors, and turn out the lights.

Such things as shooting events make the greatest news footage and gain the greatest satisfaction for those who create and execute them. We've all heard and read about them. But this text also examines other areas, such as weather or shelter in place scenarios we may become aware of. Just this last week, while I was working on this edition, a winter weather tornado tore through a neighborhood. I've never heard of a 'winter weather tornado.' They interviewed the father who saved his family, getting to the basement within seconds of hearing the familiar locomotive noise. No warning sirens, just his training and common sense. He and his family, all safe, came up from the basement and their two story home was nowhere to be found.

This edition asks that we have a plan for each and every critical event that may come our way, and to think through what our responsibilities are. But the main focus of this book is to allow you to prepare yourself, your own mind, as to what you will do when the day turns really bad and I don't mean you forgot to restock your work refrigerator with creamer and all you have as a backup is that powdered stuff with an expiration date two years ago. Sure, you'll use it, it's all you have—I would, but a little planning beforehand would have avoided you using it.

As a former law enforcement instructor making the transition to education and now to the general business community, I responded sometimes with a dumbfounded look at some of the safety issues I found in those arenas. More so there than in the business world, although you could say schools and their administrators are a type of business. In all my classes, in discussions with teachers, staff and even district administrations, I found it hard to believe the mindset—the lack of serious consideration about events like these. Unfortunately, I found that in some parts of the business world as well. It seemed especially strange after Columbine, which took fictional horror movies and made them a reality in our lives. But that was a long time ago and a lot of people have died since. We need to get better. We put on a seat belt when we get in our vehicles, not expecting an accident, but in case one shows up. Why would we not at least think about the kinds of things I talk about here?

Why forty-seven seconds? Why that specific amount of time? Who came up with that random number?

I did.

That is the time I kept averaging in preparing my own room—my own work space. Once the alert sounded, I went counter-clockwise to button up my room, turn off the lights, shut down computers, close the blinds, make the music stop, and get thirty students with hormones and afternoon body odor stink tucked away, along with their back-

> I trained as if it was real.
>
> It wasn't any better or any worse. It just was.

packs, into a corner space the size of my shower. Then, giving them a *"If I hear one sound I will set you on fire myself"* face, I take my place next to the door, which I've locked from the outside. I uncap a pen, holding it in my fist with the ballpoint sticking out between fingers three and four as a homemade shank. Every time, every time, every time I practiced with the students, I practiced myself, like I did in law enforcement. Every time, I was within a second or two of that 47-second time. I trained as if it was real. *We will play like we practice,* you will also read in this book. The last step was always leaning against the wall next to the door, closing my eyes for a moment, taking a deep breath, and letting it out slow. It was the same thing I had done for decades. It wasn't any better or any worse. It just was.

> **When you are operating in a high-stress environment, your body will work just fine, but maybe not in the way you'd like it to.**

I remember doing a search warrant on an electroplating facility in Tucson, Arizona once. Nasty places, electroplating facilities—worse than drug labs because, even though many of the chemicals are the same, they are in bulk. When they mix, you get gases and chemicals that can kill you slowly or quickly, then blow you up, along with the neighborhood. When we did warrants like that there were two things we considered in pre-planning: what is the route to the nearest hospital that can treat toxic exposure like what we would be exposed to, and where is the fire department staging so they can come rescue the cops. But everyone knew by the time the fire department got there, it would be nothing much more than a recovery operation, making sure they found all the pieces of the sheep dogs to give back to the families.

Search warrants like these brought with them new challenges. We had to clear a building that had a constant toxic cloud in it. Drug labs had something similar only usually in smaller amounts, but then they might have booby traps. We'd find tanks of five hundred gallons of some chemical, held together by rusted steel bands because it was bulging and the owner didn't want to buy a new tank. They sat next to tanks of equal size with another chemical that, when mixed with the first, would react—badly. In the meantime, there were people, in the building who had warrants for bad things and had no desire to go back to prison—at any cost. We had chemical suits on, duct-taped shut, with a compressed air tank of three thousand pounds per square inch, and guns strapped to our hips. We'd be trying to find the bad men without getting into a gun fight, and definitely without sending a round down

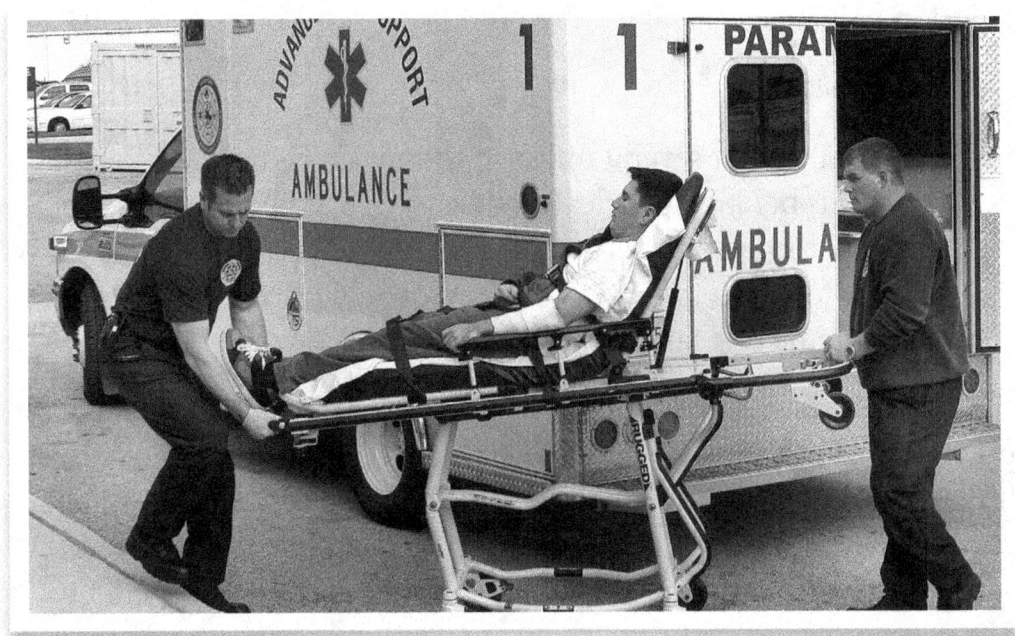

range into that bulging piece of crap they called a 'dip tank.'

When we finally settled in and came out, the paramedics took our vitals. When they took mine, well, let's just say it was interesting. When you are operating in a high-stress environment, your body will work just fine, but maybe not the way you'd like it to. If it's not trained to do otherwise, it will do what it is designed to do—stop and wait for orders. It cannot tell the difference between good stress—like that moment right before Sandra Broncowski opened the front door for you to pick her up for the Christmas Formal, and someone trying to shoot you in a hallway. If no orders come, then it will sit there until the vitals come back in to play and your brain has blood flowing to it again.

That is what this book is about, training your brain, loading that computer with information so when you and your colleagues are faced with tasks like saving your life and the lives of a bunch of co-workers, you are at least in the game. This book is short, and hopefully, if I did my job well, easy to access and enjoyable to read. There are quick reference pages and notes that you can turn to if your job site doesn't have something like it already. You can turn to that page and at least be given suggestions about what to do, somewhere to start, so you and anyone around you can see the end of the day, or if you are the night shift, see the sunrise. If I did my job well, your brain will load data and save

The point is, you are training so you will know what to do from muscle memory.

it, just in case it needs it at a pulse of high anxiety (Bourne Jr, 2003).

Just in case.

We will talk about several different things which business personnel, whom this book is specifically addressed to, could face at some point. I think the fact is, this book works for the corporate world. Easy to read, easy to put in to service, and reasonably priced. I've even used this for my home and family.

From lockdowns to evacuations and weather events, this book will provide you with valuable tools, assembled in a way you can readily use if the day starts to go really bad. That forty-seven second time might change. Maybe you will make your work area secure in thirty-eight seconds. Maybe it takes you fifty-two seconds, a few seconds either way. The point is, you are training so that you will know what to do from muscle memory. You are acting in a manner that you are familiar with. What happens on the other side of your secured door you probably won't have any control over, but your office or your space is yours. You know it better than anyone and believing you can survive that day is what you are mentally and physically training for. If you have other people in your room, they are yours as well. If you live, chances are they will live too.

Those tools I mentioned, are already in you. You have a brain—you are training your brain to tap in to this new training and apply that common sense I mentioned earlier. You have a skill set no one else has and you can use that not only to your own advantage, but for the survival and safety of others. You will play like you practice!

> You are training so that you will know what to do from muscle memory.

Things to Remember:

- *You have prepared for this event.*
- *You have a plan to live out the day.*
- *You know your space better than anyone.*
- *Control your heart rate and anxiety level by trusting your skill set and training.*
- *The greatest tool you have is common sense and being able to tap it.*
- *Never get in a gunfight with a 3000psi air tank on your back.*

Thought Point:

What do you think is your greatest personal WEAKNESS? Why?

_____
_____
_____
_____
_____
_____
_____
_____
_____
_____

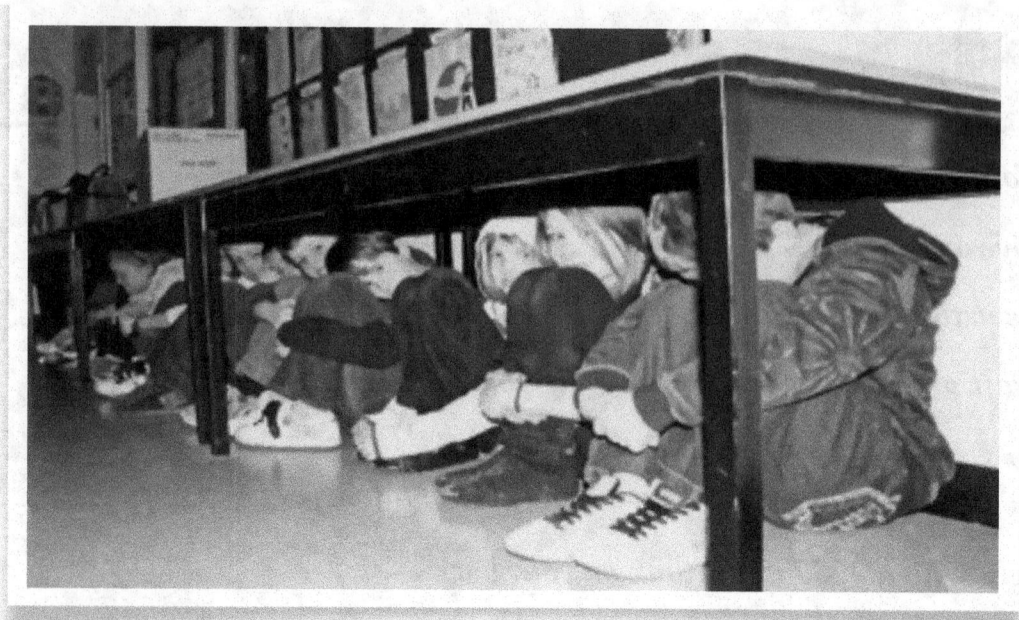

The Lockdown

Lockdown day is just going to be a bad day. In any location or job, any time you have to lock yourself in to a place with the possibility of your life being extinguished by someone you would usually only see on the TV news, is just bad. But you have to deal with it, you have to deal with the fact that you might not only be trying to make yourself safe, but a room full of colleagues, ranging from diabetics, to great grandparents. When the moment happens, ignoring it or crying about it will cause your body to do things you absolutely don't want it to do—like freeze up, or make unnecessary noise—like crying about it. It will wait for orders from the brain and without any pre-planning, ignoring the nightmare, the brain is overwhelmed by the new data and is processing just as fast as it can. But seconds are ticking off.

The simple fact is, if you don't think about these events in the quietness of a peaceful day, having to make up a bunch of stuff during a high stress, dynamically kinetic event will jeopardize you and others. By reading this book, you are doing just what you need to do. You're thinking about that really bad day and about things that might or might not happen—before they become a reality.

What do you do?

You trust your training.

There are several things we need to think about in advance. We need to think about ourselves and our abilities and what we can do, physically and mentally, to stay alive. Ask yourself: *What can 'I' do to live to see the sunset one more time?* There is a question in the back of this chapter I want you to answer for yourself as well.

Here is something we don't often hear: *As an employee, there is no requirement you have to save—anyone.*

Shock huh? How does that make you feel? Not only that, but there is no requirement for anyone to save you at risk of their own life.

"Thanks, Mark, for those words of encouragement."

Even the police are not 'required' to lay their life on the line for you or for me. But they do. It's how they're made. We cannot ask our staff to be held to that standard. But sometimes we do. We usually respond to an event with a desire to help, even at risking our own lives. That is who most of us are. We need to know what we can do in such a moment, then practice it and rehearse it. Oh, and equally as important, what we can't do. We don't want to try to figure it out when our pulse is screamingly high and we can't come up with our own birthdate.

A 'Lockdown' alert almost always means there is someone—a teen, a former employee, a current employee, someone who has no connection to the business sometimes, who is in the process of killing people and they just haven't gotten to you—yet. It doesn't make any difference if they are rich or poor, tall or short, young or old. Predicting them would be about as likely as running the roulette table at Caesar's Palace. Some experts can come up with a formula to categorize them, maybe make them more visible, but frankly it won't do you any good on this day. **This day needs to be a day of reaction, instinct, luck, and common sense.**

The randomness of the shooter is not so random. We will talk about the 'Boogeyman' later, but this just ties in well here. They are at your business with specific issues of anger, targeted at some group. Your three person real estate office is on their list. Maybe you work at a ware-

> You can discover what your enemy fears most by observing the means he uses to frighten you.
>
> — Eric Hoffer
> (1902-1983)

house, or a doctor's office, or a church—same play, different stage. They know they will be on the news, and make the headlines. They are people who actually know they will probably die, but really don't care. Someone not afraid of dying is a scary individual. They know they will die, actually desire it, so that the pain they are feeling will stop or the voices in their head, or the justice they think they will be handing out. They have a cause they are willing to die for. Drugs of some kind are almost always in their system.

What are you going to do?
What are the strengths you can employ?
What weaknesses of yours do you want to minimize?

Like usually you are a runner and fit, but you broke your leg and have to use one of those scooters. Or, you are morbidly obese and have trouble even walking. You have to deal with your own physical status.

> In this chapter you will be asked questions you have probably neve been asked before.

In this chapter, you will be asked questions you have probably never been asked before. They can apply to some of the other topics in this book as well. Later in the book, we will discuss who these people are who want to bring this nightmare to your door. Their intent can run a spectrum from an upset, hormonal student, to a sociopath who loves the idea of spreading terror just before they kill you. Most often they are male. And here is the worst and to me, the scariest part: They are sane. That outlook might be argued among my colleagues, but what I mean is they are cognitively rational, thinking human beings. They have a twisted mission but, for the most part, they are mentally together. Scary.

For some businesses of any size, like a warehouse, during a lockdown, we hear an announcement, which should be completely different from the evacuation alarm. It should be a warm body talking to us. It might not be the shop foreman, or manager, because they might have been a target and be incapacitated. In some businesses, the offices are lined up like a walking shooting gallery and one office and victim leads to the next, but we should hear an announcement and it should be definitive:

"Attention, attention, this is a lockdown, this is a lockdown."

That might be all you hear. Even worse, the announcement might be a colleague running and screaming. That's all you need. You have prepped yourself. If you supervise anyone and you initiate your plan, it could be a drill, but it's not. All your thoughts are now to play like you practiced, maybe you only did it in your mind. For most of American businesses, you will be close enough to the event to see it start. You don't need an announcement. It just showed up.

The first thing you do is stop what you're doing, and secure yourself in a room or closet, or refrigerator, some room or space you can get to or if you can run—run!

Your 'forty-seven second clock' just started. Once you secure your door, no one gets in unless they have a key or they force their way in. If you know a colleague or even you are in the restroom, that is now your place. Stay there if you can and secure yourself. You are on your own. ***Crawl up on the toilet, lock the stall door if you can. Get small and get real quiet.***

If you you're in a space with a door to lock, don't open it. At least I tell you not to open it. It is your call. But here is a reason why not to:

During a school shooting, a teacher had her class get small and quiet. They were in a lockdown, and it was real. There was a knocking on the door. One of her students was begging to be let in. The teacher didn't do what she so wanted to do. Her training kept her from it. On the other side of the door, the killer had a girl from that room and had instructed her to knock and get him in or he would kill her. She tried and begged and cried. But the door didn't open. He did what he said he would do, but he didn't get the rest of the students.

If you are out in the open, or a big warehouse, run and hide if you are out in the open. If you can flee the business, do so. And call 911. Maybe there is a pre-selected Safe Haven in the business space for you to get to and secure yourself in—ask. These are usually larger rooms where several people, dozens, or even hundreds, can get into and secure—a place an employee can run to if they are caught out in the open. If it's locked, you need to have a secondary place to hide and become part of the invisible world.

The second thing to do, secure yourself against a wall, low on the

> Once you lock your door, no one gets in unless they have a key or they force their way in.
>
> Those in the restrooms are on their own.

floor, away as best you can from any 'sight lines,' that is, anywhere a shooter might be able to see in to your space and see if anyone is there. If you have curtains, close them. Turn off the lights and computers. 'Get small and get quiet.' The perfect place is low with backs to a brick wall with no ability for the hiding place to be seen from that window. Which may mean under that same window the shooter might be looking through.

Under NO circumstances should you put a colored card out under the door to indicate your status—a method used years ago and, unfortunately still used in some locations. Under that system, green means 'all good' and Red means 'we have a problem.' The problem is, there will be no one there to see it or do anything about it, except the shooter. They will see the card, in front of a door to a room they thought was empty—you got small and quiet, remember? Now those bad people have good people they can attack. **The whole goal is to disappear.**

With our changing communities, you might have colleagues from other countries who know this is a bad thing because they lived it. It was part of their past to have soldiers or militia or bandits enter their village or housing complex or neighborhood and murder anyone they found or select individuals to send a message. These events could trigger these people who are truly suffering from some form of post-traumatic stress, PTSD, and begin to panic. If they see calm in you, it will help keep them be calm. It will help everyone—even yourself. Your insides will be screaming, but your visual demeanor will calm the room. All of a sudden, you are the person they look to for assurance.

'Mark, uh, I don't want to be that person. I don't want to.'

No one does. This event has you witnessing and experiencing murder. It isn't a movie, it's real. But now, you have an idea what to do, because you've at least thought about it. ***If you can't find it in you, fake it.*** There is no other way. You need to buy time, about fifteen to twenty minutes, until the cavalry—the police—get there.

Your day, your life, comes down to that window of time. If you work in a store which may employ young teens, no cell phones and no texting, unless it's 911. Believe it or not, teens and even adults

If you have curtains, close them. Turn off the lights and computers.

'Get small and get quiet.'

who don't know anything else to do will text others— family, friends, their cousin in Pittsburgh and it will go something like this:

"S'up?"

"Nothin', s'up wit u?"

"Stupid Lockdown."

"Really? Lame."

"Yeah, they do this every month."

"Double lame."

Problem is, every time they hit a key or get a text, it makes a noise, a vibration at the minimum, and believe it or not, Mr. Crazy Eyes, outside the room—the one who has been doing crystal meth for the last five days and hasn't slept—can hear that noise through the wall or door. That's all he/she needs to start shooting.

If you have your cell phone, keep it near you. If you carry it in a purse, or bag, keep it in your possession and switch it to silent mode. It is your only means of communication with the outside world where help is coming. DON'T call the office and ask 'Hey, is this real? I got a forklift pallet I'm moving here and I…."

You need to buy time, about fifteen to twenty minutes until the cavalry (the police) can get there.

Practice drills are necessary, even to a limited degree. These things always happen at the most inopportune time. In Arizona, for example, it is possible to have a Shelter-in-Place or even a lockdown as a quick response to some weather event. In your area, it might mean getting under a desk or behind some kind of barricade. Hopefully, if your company has any size to it, an administrator will come on the PA and clarify which of these courses it is. For this training; however, a Lockdown means someone wants to do us harm. No one except those who need to know should realize which event is practice and what is real. For a staff member, they are ALL real. We will play like we practice and if we do it well, we live out the day.

Major corporations or large businesses are a little different, just because of their size. They are more inclined to have employees coming and going. While some event may be happening in the showroom, the employees in the back lot, warehouse, or out buildings have no clue.

Word has got to get to them. Public address systems are probably the quickest. Check where you work and see what is available and ask your management.

Virginia Polytechnic Institute and State University (Virginia Tech) in 2007 had their event and on chunks of the campus people were still going to class and didn't know anything about it. Thirty-two people died in that event, second only to the Orlando nightclub killings in 2016 and Mandalay Bay Resort in Las Vegas killing sixty people and injuring well over 800. Yes, even in events like this you need to ask yourself, *"What do I do if…."* In all of these, police were there in minutes but then had to fight their way inside the buildings to get to the shooter.

Remember, only one of two types of people will come through that door and you need to be ready. If the police come, you will know it's them. They might even have a key to allow access. If it is the attacker, well, you need to be ready for that as well.

What does your location already have as far as a plan? Is there one printed with some of these steps listed that you can keep handy? Remembering a list will be good, but don't depend on it. That list, if you miss one, it could cause you to freeze. 'Wait, I did one, two and, what the heck was three!!?'

Do you have a secondary escape route in case you need to leave and cannot leave the regular way? The examples are endless and probably the biggest one is the Twin Towers on September 11th in New York. Some people, few but some, actually made it down from the upper floors passed the impact area of the exploding planes which torpedoed through the building, causing it to eventually fail. There was no shooter, but an attack was clear. At Columbine High School, students were throwing themselves out of second story windows to escape.

Can you do that? Can you jump from a higher floor? Obviously, in New York, some jumped to escape the alternate death by fire. But how about a second story to escape a shooter?

What are you able to do? Can you run? Fight?

Can the windows even open? In modern buildings, they are often not able to. If they don't open, can they be broken? Many are safety

> During the Lockdown, bad things are happening outside your office or work area.
>
> You have command of your space and how you will manage possibly hours of such a security level.

glass which means if you have to go out the window you will be beating on it with anything you can to try to break it. Then, what are you going to use to get from any floor other than the first, to the ground?

Like I said, it's a bad day.

Sometimes, our priorities need to be updated. I've had people tell me *that won't happen here.* I've had managers tell me they only train for those things they are required to train for by the government, like fire drills. The number of people who have died in a school-related fire, for example, in the last thirty years is almost zero. One person, and it was a heart attack we will mention later. But when you look at things like shooter events, or even weather, the numbers go way up to well over a hundred killed and hundreds of thousands seriously hurt by violence every year—hundreds of thousands. Between the years 2007-2012, 84 people were killed—in just four events *(USDOJ)*. At the time of this writing in the first half of 2022, there have been 153 killings in mass murder type attacks. And that number is going up. Mandalay Bay which I used as an example earlier took the numbers in to orbit including those not killed but injured, over 800.

The lockdown is your Alamo. Maybe that was a bad analogy. Everyone died at the Alamo, but the idea is you need to hold on for a while—alone. Help is coming but since the shooting at Columbine High School in April, 1999, police have changed their tactics and instead of coming to rescue you, they are going to the threat first. They can't get to you without first making the shooter or attacker stop the attack. You have to survive until they do that part of their job. You have to hold on.

Here comes the hard question, and this course is meant to begin the thought process:

What are you willing to do to live?

Whether you are a brand new employee at eighteen years old, or you are in your last year before your retirement, a diabetic with two bad hips, you need to think about what you can do to stay alive.

That thought, that answer may determine whether you see another sunset or not.

> What does your location already have as far as a plan? Is there one printed with some of the steps listed that you can keep handy?

Forty-Seven Seconds

Things to Remember:

- *As soon as the announcement for a lockdown is made, the work process ends.*
- *Begin to secure your room or work area.*
- *Outside activities quickly move to a secure place*
- *Get workers small and quiet and out of sight lines from any outside view.*
- *Cell phones off.*
- *Make the room/space look abandoned.*

Thought Point:

Close your eyes and picture one of your colleagues pounding on your door, pleading with you to let them in. What are you going to do? Why?

_____
_____
_____
_____
_____
_____
_____
_____

Mark Williams

Shelter-in-Place

*The superior man, when resting in safety,
does not forget that danger may come.*

When in a state of security, he does not forget the possibility of ruin.

When all is orderly, he does not forget that disorder may come.

Thus his person is not endangered,

and his States and all their clans are preserved.

Confucius (551 BC – 479 BC)

I love this quote.

Time and time again I have heard colleagues, administrators, and staff say, "Oh, that won't happen here." Whether we are talking about a violent event such as a shooting, or a weather event, or a gas leak, or a plane flying into the floor right below us, it will happen.

It, whatever it is, is not likely to happen anywhere. But it will happen somewhere and it can happen at any school, business, temple, hospital, restaurant, subway or public facility—even your home. Schools, and places of worship being considered 'soft targets,' are vulnerable to someone wanting to make a point and inflict psychological harm (Ronningen, 2012). The idea that only businesses in a bad part of town will have these types of violence is statistically erroneous. This last two years saw major cities burned and pillaged by organized groups. After a while, the daily events didn't even make the news.

We are now in an era of violence where groups such as ISS, Antifa, or any other alphabet soup mix of letters of groups are being added to the mix and will look at these sights as excellent targets and, frankly, they are perfect for the goal these groups want to achieve. They will get lots of news exposure.

Like buying car insurance, you hope you don't get in an accident, but you know someday it will happen. A car accident event will happen every 17.9 years (Troup, 2011). The odds of dying by being shot is a little over 1 in 24,000. Actually, those are pretty good odds (the Economist).

Some businesses, schools, or places of employment, have something less than a lockdown and call this level 'Shelter-in-Place'. It is a level of preparation where staff need to be aware of something around their facility, which might seek to harm them. The threat is not imminent, but it could change quickly. It doesn't even have to be a human threat. Weather could trigger the need for sheltering.

An example of this took place at a school not too long ago. The event was a robbery of a local store nearby and the school resource officer was monitoring the police radio traffic as he always did. The suspects left the store after they had robbed it and were driving down the street, near the school.

At this Shelter-in-Place level, the work processes keep going, but staff began preparing to escalate to a full lockdown or maybe an evacuation in response to other events which might dictate securing of personnel inside a building or evacuating from it. For a weather event, employees could start to prepare to leave or find those hardened safe points inside their work area to move to.

> A 'Shelter In Place' is a security level less restrictive than a Lockdown.
>
> ...It's activation could be in response to preparing for an actual Lockdown...

After hearing a Shelter In Place announcement, employees should begin to prep their work areas to escalate to a full lockdown.

A Shelter-in-Place is a security level less restrictive than a lockdown. Staff are still working. Its activation could be in response to preparing for a possible lockdown, coming out of a lockdown, weather condition, local issues like a gas leak, or some other event, for which management deems it necessary to provide shelter behind secured doors and walls. It can be used prior to an escalation of a threat or as the threat decreases, a step down, allowing work to recover from a full lockdown, restrooms used, etc. It would be on a case by case basis and usually the office manager or their designee is calling the threat level. In the Mid-West where tornadoes just show up uninvited, this is a useful tool. A sighting might be in the next town over and staff may prepare to head for shelter, the Shelter in Place helps them get there. Some of the things staffers can manage not to do are:

- *You don't need to call the office.* If we flood the office with calls, it contorts their ability to do what they need to do.

- *You don't need to text anyone* unless you are warning them of what is happening and for them to take shelter.

- *You don't need to text or call home*, depending. There will be plenty of time for that.

- *You don't need to know what is going on.* (This one is hard!)

You just need to do what you were trained to do. This may sound somewhat hard and 'rude' but imagine what is going on in the office, with whomever is responsible for your office complex. They are busy with coordinating the whole thing and their one goal is to make people safe. Time is not a luxury in these moments; it is an adversary. If things are not moving quickly to security, it could result in people getting caught out in the open and exposed to harm. Your call, your desire to know more than you need to, could result in more confusion—even harm to others. After hearing the Shelter in Place announcement, staff should prepare for an escalation or de-escalation in the threat level.

Like we said, you begin to prep your space but may continue to work. No need to not finish Mrs. Lowenstein's tooth extraction, but while you are drilling, you could make sure things in your area or secure. Shelter in Place could mean someone harmful has the potential of coming on to our work site as they drive away from the robbery they just pulled. That means we need to start preparing for what trouble may come. It could also mean something that was meant to harm us is passing, or has just passed, and we can step down from a Lockdown to something less restrictive.

Don't forget weather, really the greater threat. We can return to some sense of normalcy. Administrators will want to return the work area to peace and quiet as soon as possible.

Have a plan for yourself and anyone around you. Is there a way you can have snacks, games, something for you to occupy yourself for long periods of time quietly during a Shelter-in-Place? An emergency restroom facility is not needed for a Shelter-in-Place if the restroom is close enough— but remember it could change from a sheltering to a lockdown, and if it escalates to a lockdown, they need to stay there in the restroom and shelter themselves in the stall, don't come back to the room. It should be locked.

Shelter-in-Place is precautionary, but it is just a level down from a lockdown. It is to buy you a little bit of time. A Shelter-in-Place could be called, for example, if the robbery suspects I mentioned earlier begins to drive down a street which leads past your business or school or place of worship. The School Resource Officer, maybe monitoring police channels, might hear the radio traffic and advise the principal, who decides to play it safe and call for shelter. The officer later advises

Your response is... prepare for an escalation or de-escalation in the threat level.

that the suspects have passed the school and the principal releases the students and staff from the Shelter-in-Place level.

Not much changed in the work area, but precious seconds were saved. Your work space isn't much different. In that particular case of the robbery, it would have taken the suspects 32 seconds to make a right turn and drive on to campus and into the heart of the classrooms. Remember what I said up front: It routinely takes 47 seconds for me to prep and lockdown my room?

I know. I timed both.

Things to Remember:

- *When a Shelter-in-Place is called, begin to secure your area as you would for a lockdown.*

- *The work process keeps going for most of the work site.*

- *Activities outside start to find a way in to a more secure, protected setting.*

- *Allow employees who were away from their offices to return.*

- *Doors do not need to be locked unless your common sense tells you to.*

- *With regards to your snacks, this situation totally justifies your favorite, rather than your diet-goo bar.*

Mark Williams

Thought Point:

Have you trained your employees and staff in what they should do in the restroom or out on campus if a Shelter-in-Place is called? What can you say to help them clarify their actions?

_____
_____
_____
_____
_____
_____
_____
_____
_____
_____
_____
_____
_____
_____
_____
_____
_____

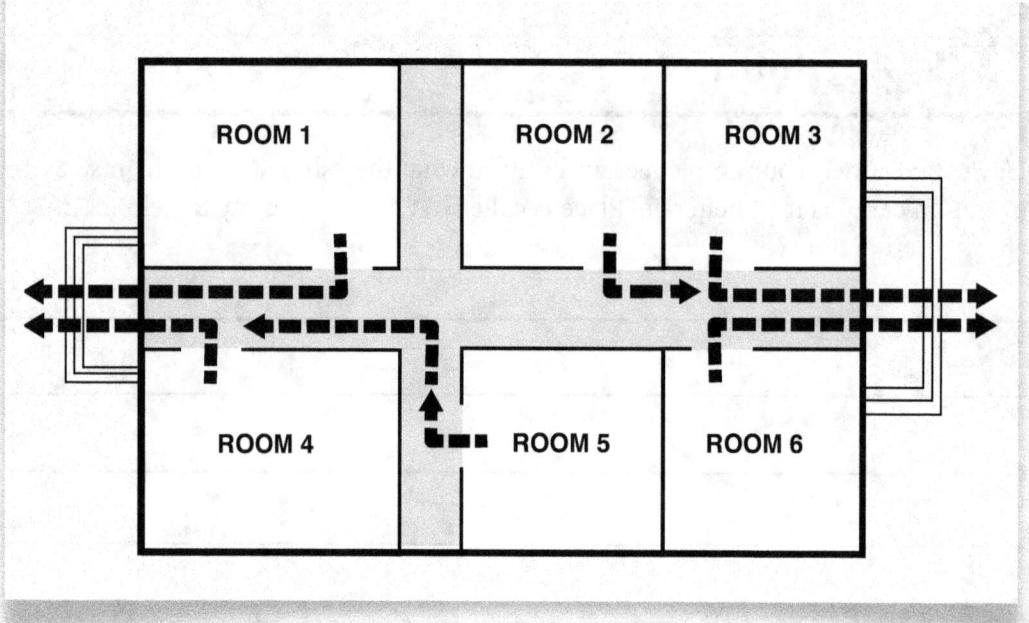

The Evacuation

A goal without a plan is just a wish.

-**Antoine de Saint-Exupery (1900 – 1944)**

When I was growing up, evacuations use to be called 'fire drills,' because there really was nothing greater than the fear of being burned alive while trapped in a classroom or a confined space. Other than having your child burning alive while trapped in a classroom, there was nothing else we, as parents, could not save them from. We also had 'duck and cover' drills so we would all survive a nuclear event, but someone woke up one day and realized that was pretty stupid, since we were all going to be fried toast in a five-mile wide hole anyway, at least in Phoenix, where I grew up. When the Cold War finally waned, strategic reports released from the former Soviet Union showed the Metro Phoenix area, with all its airports, nuclear power plants, and at the time, two Air Force bases, had been targeted with five individual Soviet warheads.

We could duck and cover all day long, but by the end of the day, if a nuclear war ever took place, the Valley of the Sun would be no more —occupied only by the hearty oleander and, of course, the cockroach. But the fire drill was good. It was a good idea to walk through a plan on how to herd a bunch of kids outside during a real fire. Before 9/11, the Twin Towers in New York actually practiced escaping those buildings. There was never a practice to evacuate from a building that was cut in two, it was always a fire, but they practiced getting all the thousands of people out and to the street safely. That played a huge roll in saving lives that day.

Today it could be a gas leak, some chemical issue, or many things other than fire, since most of the things in our work space are now fire resistant and there are enough sprinkler heads in that same space where a fear of drowning standing up is the better possibility. You need to go back years to find a fire with 10 or more deaths at a school (NFPA). In 1958, Our Lady of Angels School in Chicago had a fire with 95 deaths. Since then, and just as a snap shot, from 2009 to 2013 there was one fatality in a school-related fire, and whether that death was directly related to the fire or some other health issue the victim may have had, such as a heart attack. The point is—times have changed.

At the time of the writing, the Bronx had an apartment fire with seventeen casualties. It was a poster example of what not to do, where not to live, and how one can really get trapped and die from fire and smoke, especially if they did not take the time to ask themselves how to get out of a place they were not familiar with. I don't think that will be our issue here, in your space. Still, it isn't a bad idea to look around and make sure you have some good safety equipment and an evacuation plan in your room, or close by. This is a great idea for your home. Do your kids know what to do and how to get out without your help? Here is a question to start off this chapter: Do you have a fire evacuation sign by your door or near it?

I don't think that will be our issue here, in your space. Still, it isn't a bad idea to look around and make sure you have some good safety equipment and an evacuation plan in your room, or close by.

... do you have a fire evacuation sign by your door or near it?

Forty-Seven Seconds

Here is a question to start off this chapter: Do you have a fire evacuation sign by your door or near it?

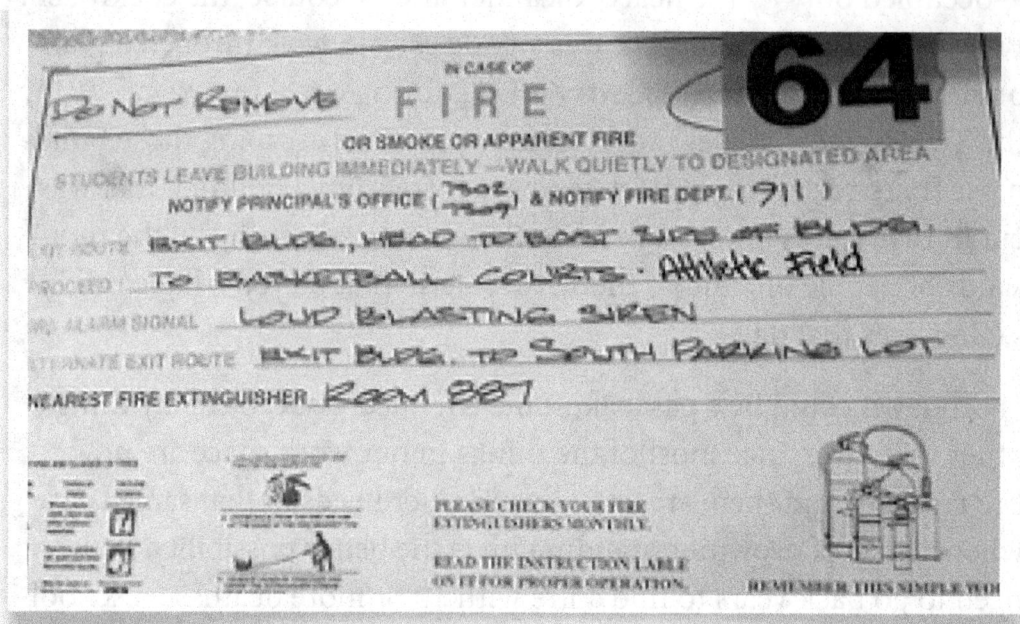

Training, training, training is the key. Training in advance.

There are different types of signs that describe how to get out and where to go, and most states and municipalities have requirements for them to be placed near the exit door. If you don't have one like it, ask your work administrator where you can get one and where you are to go in the event of an emergency. Now, this is usually for large facilities. You don't really need one if you can see the exit to the hamburger restaurant you own. But sometimes your work exit leads to a larger section of the building and in the craziness of an evacuation, you want to know which way to turn. How about a fire sign in your own home? In the heat of the moment, even you might not think clearly where to turn. You can place it on the back of your child's room door. Even your door.

Training, training, training, is the key. Training in advance. You do not want to be reading this sign to find out where to go while your room or building is filling with gas from the natural gas leak in Mrs. Libostein's Hat Shop next door.

On the sign I'm referring to, you will see the number '64' on the top right hand corner. There is a corresponding number on the fence or some other rallying point outside, which is where this particular room evacuates to.

The directions on the sign take you to that particular fence or other safe location. This is very helpful if you have a large property and want your employees out and away from any outside threats like gas or access for emergency vehicles. In the picture, the office who owns this location, evacuates to that location. Maybe it's a color or some other indicator. The point is, if you are *here*, you are to go *there*.

Evacuations should be practiced at least every six months, or even quarterly. You rehearse these and it might even save you on company insurance. When the Towers fell in New York on September 11th, employees of those buildings had actually trained in evacuating their buildings (World, 2003). No one ever imagined a jet plane full of fuel would fly in to their building, but I am not sure you can over-train with such events. The training they had done in advance got everyone under the impact floors out. Floor captains and section leaders relied on their training as it kicked in for the real event and their response saved thousands.

You might get a new employee who has no idea where to go until he or she is told or shown. All employees should know where their evacuation site is for that particular work location. An employee needs to know the best way to do this is to practice. You, as an employer, want to account for everyone. The reason is if one is found missing, a decision needs to be made by the responding fire department whether to go look for them. An unnecessary risk if they are safe but in the wrong place.

Situational awareness (Ray, 2012) is a term we will use here.

Emergency responders and the military are acutely aware of this term. Being aware of your surroundings and doing so before you actually need to know and implement those escape plans is common sense and yet one we don't seem to use much. Waiting for someone else to tell you to leave when common sense is telling you to move is deadly.

Let me give you an example: How many of you get on a plane, sit down, and then look for the nearest exit and actually imagine leaving your seat with your eyes closed (because we all know it will be dark and smoky) and see ourselves getting up from our seat, turning left or right, counting the number of rows by feel as we move to the exit? You don't fly? Okay, how about a city bus or train? Can you find the escape door? Do you know how to pull the release handle on the roof hatch of the bus which is turned over—in the lake—and is sinking—with your eyes

> All employees should know where their evacuation site is for that particular work location.

Forty-Seven Seconds

Waiting for someone else to tell you to leave when common sense is telling you to move is deadly.

shut? Time to go, to evacuate, is when the alarm sounds or if you hear no alarm and you find or know something is wrong.

As you leave, if you know where the pull switches are, activate them while you leave and pass the word as best you can. It is not uncommon to have building alarm systems not be fully functioning. One area might hear the alarm while another close area is not going off. Some systems can be activated in zones. You might not want the entire building to empty, just a wing of it. This can often be controlled by the administrator, security, or maintenance personnel who have access to it, but just because you are not 'told' to leave doesn't mean you ignore the world around you.

Use your training and common sense.

"Well, I don't know if I should? I mean, it isn't really my job."

I have heard this comment—from supposedly educated people. Problem is, education does not always equal common sense. Don't worry, it's in every profession. What would you do? The fact is, it is everyone's job.

I will say something here that probably is not too politically correct, but oh well, it's my book.

Some of the dumbest people I have ever known have been highly educated individuals and some of the smartest have been barely high school grads. I think the reason for that is maybe the high school grads had to rely on their common sense and life skills more than the others. The educated seem to quote a book they read once, like you might use mine. Sometimes, that book might have been written by someone who, again, has virtually no life experience, they're just regurgitating book knowledge. If that is the case, if you use my book as a conversation piece while you sip wine at the museum for a new opening, then quote the most important part. I'll even bold it and put it in quotes: *"Common sense will save you."*

Your job will advise you whether to leave your door unlocked or not. Responding fire crews want the doors unlocked which means have employees take their personal items as well, to minimize items that might be stolen by someone lingering behind. Yes, items can 'disappear.' Believe it or not, not all staff are trustworthy and some actually take advantage of the abandoned building to go back and see what they can find. Look around in your work space. How many sprinklers do you see in the ceiling? In rooms I have been in, I have seen as many as five. The work areas are made now with fire retardant material and the fire marshal conducts annual inspections, making sure the rooms and spaces are safe and up to fire code. The American public demands their children are safe in schools, and it will be, hopefully, a far off day, when any of our children die in a fire. The adult work space should be the same. Drowning from the sprinklers working well is another issue, but they should be safe from fire. The workplace, well, that can be a different matter. Companies sometimes are short sighted and relax their preparedness—for whatever reason, none of them are good.

Do you have a fire extinguisher in your room? You might not be required to have one, but if you do, facility maintenance personnel should check annually or semi-annually and make sure it's charged. This is something you can do as well. There is a little dial on it. Read it and see what it says. If it is low, notify your administrator about it. A fire extinguisher is a very large paper weight if it does not function.

In Arizona as I think in most states, the fire code pushes places to practice an evacuation every month (Arizona, 2016). There are other things which can generate an evacuation, natural gas for example or in some businesses, there are chemicals that simply don't react well if they are mixed, if you know what I mean. I had mentioned early in the book about electroplating shops. Those places could have chemicals mixing with other chemicals and kill you without any fire at all. Still just as lethal. These labs, if not properly maintained and watched by staff, can sometimes collect chemicals which will degrade and become toxic—or worse, shock sensitive. That means they form crystals under the lid and when you open it and hear that little grinding sound like a salt shaker lid opening, it could be the last thing you hear on this earth. Crazy stuff. A location I was at had 135 small containers in a former chemistry lab of chemicals that were mislabeled, unlabeled, or in various states of decay. A HAZMAT contractor had to come in and pack them up. That was expensive, but not nearly as expensive as their potential explosive decomposition.

Many work locations have natural gas piped to their stores or shops. It comes in via a large four-inch-diameter or larger pipe under high pressure, and is stepped-down to a lower pressure into the individual work areas. Somewhere in this line, things could go wrong and break. Gas collecting in a confined space like a room, office, or work area, gas could reach a level between the lower explosive limit or LEL and the upper explosive limit or UEL (RK, 2013) where the oxygen is too lean or

too rich. This is the sweet spot for ignition. And the ignition source can be something as mundane as turning on the light switch. Gas doesn't have to be explosive, it could simply displace the oxygen and you quietly suffocate.

This is not the kind of line that feeds gas into your family home. This is a high-pressure line feeding a building—its heating system, boilers, cafeteria, and labs. It comes out of the ground and into the meters and valves before it goes back underground to the buildings. The lines are usually protected with concrete or metal barricades but if they are hit hard enough—say, with a vehicle—they can rupture, letting high pressure, highly flammable gas cover a wide area.

Bomb threats, smoke, anything that could put life or health at risk could require the mass movement of employees to a safe area. It could require having everyone leave the area completely for some other facility away from the job site.

When that happens, you are the guide, because you're prepared. If a colleague is away from their work location, you, as their colleague, need to have taught them what to do, to not come back, but to hurry to their evacuation site and join you. Yes, leave them. You do not sacrifice an office of people for one person. Hard times call for hard choices.

Someone will make a decision whether to go look for any missing, like we just discussed. It is critical that you communicate clearly about the seriousness of the possible consequences of their actions. Otherwise, a fire fighter goes in looking for them and, right then, the confined gas ignites, killing the rescuer and leaving his or her family without a daddy or mommy, all because of poor choices that employee made. Sounds too far-fetched? Ask an emergency responder about it. They would go in a heartbeat and mention examples they have seen of this.

If there are many employees, a roster of those people for that evacuation should travel to the evacuation site. Then, role can be taken and if someone is missing you will know about it. You might even have an extra employee. Add their name to the list. You found them and that rescuer will not have to go in to find them. Some businesses have forms for this. Hopefully, an administrator will come around and get it from you, radio in the employee's name, and a decision whether to go launch a search for that person will be made. You don't go looking for the miss-

> You do not sacrifice a room or office full of people for one person.
>
> Hard times call for hard choices.

ing employee. Report that person missing so help can come to them. They may be misplaced, or on the warehouse floor overcome by fumes. If you went in to find them, you might be overcome as well.

It is here that reality sets in. If this is real and if the employee is left behind or didn't find their way out of the room, there is a possibility of injury or death. The idea is to train those employees to do it on their own, in case they are alone and there is no one to help them.

> It is here that reality sets in. Life and death. Something you never took a class on in college comes into play.

If you have a handicapped employee with mobility issues, like a wheel chair restricting movement down flights of stairs and you are on a second or higher floor, it will depend on whether you can use the elevator or not and if you or the employee has a key to access it. Sometimes, during a fire/evacuation event, the elevators are sent to the ground floor and do not function without a fire key, owned by the fire department. In this case, the business might have what is called an Area of Rescue or Refuge. You can also call the fire department and tell them where you are if you have a cell phone. Again, use common sense. At some businesses, there is a phone for staff to call for assistance from the refuge area.

There is a liability with this situation, so check with your administration. I would be willing to bet no one has asked them who stays with the employee and who goes. What does common sense say about staying at this rescue area when the building is burning? Believe it or not, how you practice will relate directly to how you play. Think about evacuating beyond the rescue area. What about the elevator? Just because they said you can't use it, doesn't mean you can't use it. Can you carry the employee down the stairs? Dragging the wheelchair behind you?

You need to think through these events and actions. Once you do, once you see how you do it in your mind, the computer has been set. You have a plan and it is a functional workable plan, in your mind. It is so much better than watching your pulse climb to 180 beats a minute while you can't come up with your own name, let alone a plan for how to get your colleague down from the fourth floor. You will not be able to improvise much when the world around you is heating up. Your brain won't allow it because it is running at a maximum capacity, so have a plan, think it through and practice it. If you escape a burning building and you and everyone gets out safe, no one will care how you did it.

Hopefully, you will practice this and it will become second nature to you. Every time you do it, practice like you will play. Fires, explosions, gas leaks, are never convenient. You need to work through shutting down your work space, making it safe, and getting out. This could determine whether people do well or get hurt. Have a plan and show your colleagues around you how to do it. The employees, if trained properly, and if they are mature enough, can do well.

Things to Remember:

- *Practice your evacuation route.*
- *Walk them out and practice taking attendance there.*
- *Look around your room and think about alternate escape routes.*
- *Is there a fire extinguisher in your room? Do you know how to use it? Is it charged?*
- *Do you have the office number in your cell phone so you can call them while you evacuate?*
- *Once on the field, notify an administrator of any missing or found students or staff.*
- *Yes, a practiced evacuation does count as an exercise day.*

Forty-Seven Seconds

Thought Point:

Can you leave someone behind, if required, to save others?

Think through that and write down your thoughts.

_____
_____
_____
_____
_____
_____
_____
_____
_____
_____
_____
_____
_____
_____
_____
_____

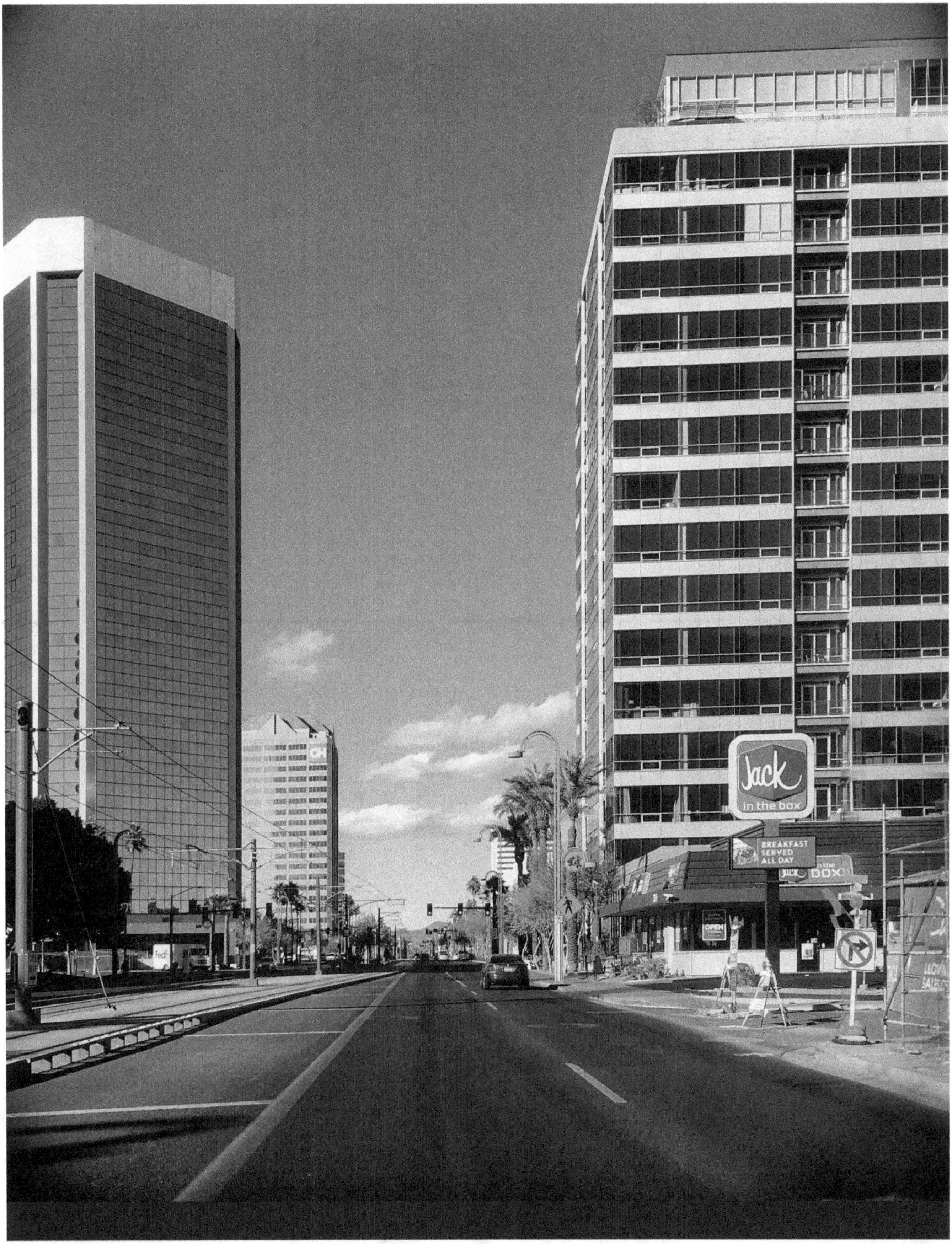

Photo © 2019 by Bob Ryan; Courtesy of Bob Ryan Creative

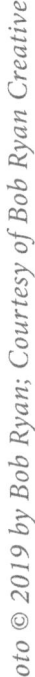

Forty-Seven Seconds

The Boogeyman

The bravest thing you can do when you are not brave

is to profess courage and act accordingly.

– Corra Harris

I am a firm believer in the Boogeyman.

Most in law enforcement and the military are. They can look like anyone—someone's kid, uncle, father, mother—just a regular person with a deep dark wish to kill you, like the two pictured above. You could try to understand them, talk to them, 'feel' for them. You can ask them to tell you why they are doing what they are doing and frankly, if it keeps you alive, keeping doing it. Chances are, though, they will look at you coldly and pull the trigger. My personal belief is there is real evil in the world and its soul desire is to kill you, your family, your friends, and your dog!

So, the idea of this entity coming in to your work environment and wanting to harm you, is not a far reach. Luckily, it is statistically small. Unfortunately, someone—someone's family, friends, or dog will be on the wrong side of this statistic, sooner or later.

There are many professionals—social workers, psychologists, counselors, who want to help parents, and families. They work to get people help as a living—the help they need. They listen to them, and care for them. It is their nature to help them. Another author on the subject of survival, Col. David Grossman, calls this group the "caring, loving, cow-puppies." It's good to care, it's good to love and nurture. Just remember, *the boogeyman does not care that you care.* The boogeyman will use your caring instinct against you—against any of us. They thrive on terror, just ask the survivors of Columbine, Red Lake, Orlando, San Bernardino, Paris, or Sandy Hook and the list goes on.

It might be someone with strong feelings towards some group or subject, just as an example. Until that moment when they choose to force that belief on the rest of us, they live here just like you and me. How they think, why they think that way, is just part of the puzzle. People will become fixated on things, let it stew in their brain pan, and then one day, they blow up the Murrah Federal Building in Oklahoma City like Timothy McVeigh and Terry Nichols.

The two were upset because two years earlier, the Branch Davidians died in a fight with Federal officers at their compound in Waco, Texas. McVeigh and Nichols picked April 19th for their truck bomb because the Davidians had their fire on, you guessed it, April 19th. Weird? Sure. Crazy? Not at all. It was planned and thought out and executed.

On a school level, the Columbine High School shooting was on April 20th, Adolph Hitler's birthday. Eric Harris and Dylan Klebold, students at the school, wanted it to rival the Oklahoma City explosion and death toll and there is a belief they wanted to associate themselves with Hitler and his murderous tendencies. Again, we like to think they were crazy—

But they weren't. They were perfectly sane.

And they live among us, right now. The police work the tips from the public and they never make the news, but they are there, right now. Every mass murderer who has made the news is making the news after they kill, not before. The police can do only so much. The courts can do only so much. Eventually, they will come in to our lives, like colliding planets.

What might happen first is anyone's guess, but let us hope we have a warning.

Survivors of these events tell of seeing others who were not only killed, but terrorized before they were killed. Many of these attackers were on some type of drug. Many had a history of being bullied or some other form of perceived outcast behavior among their peers, creating a desire to strike back. We are not going to spend a lot of time here. You don't need to know what is making them do this action or event. As we mentioned in the chapter on Lockdowns, you just need to know what to do for about twenty minutes to survive the event. Why the attacker is doing what they are doing is outside of this chapter and will be debated by sociologist, doctors, and social workers forever. How things happened after this is all over, is left for the prosecutor and coroner to figure out. You simply need to make it through for the next short period of time. Your world comes down to a ticking clock—hopefully a *silently* ticking clock, as we learned in our last chapters.

But this little bit of background on this topic may help.

There are side effects to almost anything. Looking at the related violence, many of those were conducted by individuals on some type of medication, specifically psychiatric drugs. They run the spectrum from drowsiness to hypersensitivity to hallucinations.

One day, when I was still teaching, I practiced with my class, our Lockdown procedures. As part of this exercise, I wanted to see what could be heard outside our room by a random student. I picked a girl and a boy, both sophomores, both fifteen years of age. I told them to go in the hallway outside the door and to listen and identify, if they could, anything they heard after I shut the door.

I told the class to be as quiet as possible and to turn their phones to silent and to stop giggling. Giggling, by the way, is a nervous response to fear *(Staff Mayo, 2016)*. Some of the funniest moments in my life were right before I was going to step in to something potentially very messy. When we tried to tell others after the warrant, arrest, or whatever we were doing what was so funny, they didn't get it. It was like reheated lasagna. You truly had to be there when it first came out of the oven. I was not too surprised by what I heard back from the students.

When the two students came back in, and without knowing any of the instructions given to the remaining students, they said they heard me give the instructions, then heard a phone message bell. They also heard someone jingling change and what sounded like car keys in a pocket.

That was me, making sure my phone was off in my front left pocket, with my car keys. They also said they could hear giggling. So much for getting small and getting quiet. Add to that a person on drugs making them hypersensitive to sound and you got the earmarks of a personal bad day.

We had a wall between us and the hallway. Many businesses have

> You simply need to make it through for the next short period of time. Your world comes down to a ticking clock.

no separation. Some, have a room with dozens of cubicles or an open warehouse type arrangement with nothing to block or damper the noise. When I say get small and get quiet I mean like dead quiet. Crying, whimpering, heavy breathing, shuffling of papers or whispering in to your phone to 911 becomes a high threat level.

If these young and apparently healthy kids could hear what was going on, what would happen when someone tracking with hypersensitive bat-hearing, looking for victims and having approached the door to try to open it, hears sounds of life inside? I would predict bullets would come through the wall. Hence the reason we are sitting on the floor. Hopefully the rounds go over our collective heads as they puncture the drywall. Except for me, I'm still standing there next to the door with my ball point pen in my hand. What is the saying, "never bring a knife to a gun fight?" What do you suppose Sir Sean Connery, who spoke those words in the movie *The Untouchables,* would say about bringing a *pen* to a gunfight? Yeah, I think it's a stupid idea too. But it's an idea. Yes, bullets can go through drywall—about eight rooms of drywall. It is crucial that you give the person wanting to kill you no sensual stimuli to keep them around and fixing upon you as a target. So, what are you going to do if the boogeyman gets in? Are you going to fight? Talk? Lay down? Freeze? I have made up my mind, I am going to fight the intruder with a pen. Yep, that is my weapon of choice. God help all of us. But, and this is a big but and I cannot lie, I am willing to do mighty things with that pen—if I can.

Why, oh why a pen? Well, for one thing, I always have at least one on me. Hard for me to explain why I am carrying a pair of scissors in my shirt pocket, but a pen, if I practice—and I have—I can shove that puppy right into several different target locations on the head. If I hit it just right, I can hit the on/off switch directly behind the eye socket either through the eyes, up through the sinus cavity, the pallet of the mouth or the temple—if I hit it hard enough. If I go low, I am in to the neck and the carotid artery. That is a fatal wound but not an immediate knock down wound so I will have to fight until they lose enough blood to fall. Yeah, I've thought of that sequence. So must you.

I have worked through it. Being a newly minted twenty something office worker reading this, you might be thinking this is morbid and what a terrible subject. You're right. We should never have to teach this stuff. But you snap in to a seat belt every day you drive, right? Why? In case of that accident you hope never happens. This is the same thing. Only someone wants to harm you, your co-workers, your family. The idea of someone out there having it in for us, is hard to imagine. You haven't done anything to them, but the answer is, you have. You are a symbol of something they want to end, or use to make themselves known. Your death will bring that glory—to them.

If you're not fleeing the location, you want to be small, quiet, and very very still. Hopefully, they will not have patience and will want to quench their thirst somewhere else, not in your work space. That means they move down to your neighbor's room. There is nothing you can do about that, but if it makes you feel any better, your neighbor is trying do the same thing to you. It's something the two of you can talk about later, if everything goes well. Psychiatric drugs are needed, absolutely and I just landed on this list below as an example of what we were addressing above. The two shooters in the North Hollywood shoot out, where thirteen police officers were wounded after the Bank of America was robbed, and almost two thousand rounds of ammunition were expended for about 30 minutes, were on meds, which was a reason they didn't feel the pain of the rounds they were taking, actually hitting them. As a comparison, most police gunfights are from 2-10 feet away and last under five seconds. North Hollywood was about 30 minutes. Here is just an example of a few of those shooting summaries:

Tallahassee, Florida – November 20, 2014: 31-year-old Myron May, a Florida State University alum, opened fire in the school's library, wounding three before he was shot and killed by police. ABC Action News found a half-filled prescription for the antianxiety drug Hydroxyzine in his apartment after the shooting. In addition, according to May's friends, he had seen a psychologist and had been prescribed the antidepressant Wellbutrin and the ADHD drug, Vyvanse.

He also checked himself into Mesilla Valley Hospital, a mental health center, around September of 2014. Shortly after this, his friends discovered the antipsychotic Seroquel among his prescriptions.

Yes, bullets can go through drywall— about eight rooms of drywall.

Forty-Seven Seconds

I'm not telling you this to scare you, but to give you strength.

Knowing what that boogeyman might look like, sound like, and act like takes some of that fear away.

Seattle, Washington – June 5, 2014: 26-year-old Aaron Ybarra opened fire with a shotgun at Seattle Pacific University, killing one student, and wounding two others. Ybarra planned to kill as many people as possible and then kill himself. In 2012, Ybarra reported that he had been prescribed the antidepressant Prozac and antipsychotic Risperdal. A report from his counselor in December of 2013 said that he was taking Prozac at the time and planned to continue to meet with his psychiatrist and therapist as needed.

Columbine, Colorado – April 20, 1999: 18-year-old Eric Harris and his accomplice, Dylan Klebold, killed 12 students and a teacher and wounded 26 others before killing themselves. Harris was on the antidepressant Luvox. Klebold's medical records remain sealed. Both shooters had been in anger-management classes and had undergone counseling. Harris had been seeing a psychiatrist before the shooting *(School Shooters)*.

I'm not telling you this to scare you, but to give you strength. Fear more often results from too little knowledge rather than too much of it. Knowing what that boogeyman might look like, sound like, and act like takes some of that fear away. Kind of like watching a scary movie in the sun light. Sure, it's scary, but you can see stuff coming from down the hallway because, well, it's in the daytime and no zombies come down a hallway during the day in full sunlight.

Everyone knows that.

I guess the last point is, Evil can look like the person next door. John Wayne Gacy was the person next door. Your ability to see that person is limited. Your preparedness is not.

Things to Remember:

- *Many of those involved in these types of crimes are on some form of drug or medication.*
- *Bullets, often a random spray of bullets, can go through most walls other than brick or block.*
- *Getting small and getting quiet is critical.*
- *Common sense tells us the more we are quiet, the better off we are.*
- *If the door is breached and the boogeyman comes in, what are you going to do?*
- *No, you don't have to join a gym to improve your odds, but it probably wouldn't hurt either.*

Forty-Seven Seconds

Thought Point:

Your workplace is in a lockdown. You've heard what sounds like gunfire. Or a shooter simply walks into your place of business and begins to shoot people. What are you going to do?

_____
_____
_____
_____
_____
_____
_____
_____
_____
_____
_____
_____
_____
_____
_____

The Cavalry

A hero is no braver than an ordinary man,
but he is brave five minutes longer.
-Ralph Waldo Emerson (1803 – 1882)

This is one of my other favorite quotes of all time. Each of us is a hero, or can be. Not that we seek it out. Heroes don't do that. It can just happen from situations we find ourselves in. For about twenty minutes, we need to hang on to life, hopefully, holding others up while we hold on ourselves. While we hunker down and work from inside. Sheep dogs are ramping up.

Among their peers, law enforcement are known as sheep dogs.

There is a saying about sheep dogs:

The sheep don't like them because they remind them of the threat of the wolf and their own vulnerability. The wolf doesn't like them because they keep them from the sheep.

Just because I'm shot doesnt mean I'm dead, nor does it mean I'm out of the fight.

So, they are standing alone between the wolf and the sheep, waiting for the day the wolf decides to test them both. The sheep dogs, when they hear the cry of sheep, will arrive. The magic of law enforcement is they always win—always. We just have to give them time.

We ended the last chapter with a question that most people tend to leave blank when I send out my 'What would you do?' situational survey. They have never thought about it. Is it a time to talk or act more aggressively? If I act, will I get hurt? I think anyone in law enforcement or the military, would tell you if you asked that last question to yourself during one of these events, you would freeze. Here is the answer, just so you know and can load that into your brain pan:

Yes, yes you will get hurt. This event will very probably cause you to also hurt something—or someone. Maybe it's an ankle or a muscle pull. Maybe my pen idea, having to get me in so close I can smell the shooter's breath, will probably get me hurt. My age doesn't do me any favors except knowledge and experience. But just because I get hurt doesn't mean I am dead, nor does it mean I am out of the fight. There. Now, deal with it, because if you don't, based on what was given to you in the situation, you and apparently many others are going to die.

When an event—a shooter, or some other form of high level threat happens on business grounds, night clubs, hospitals, temples, or other "soft target" locations—there is a plan by law enforcement in place to get to you quickly. Since Columbine, law enforcement has trained extensively in executing those responses. Columbine was the wake up call to a new threat.

Until Columbine, as we stated earlier, police would arrive with their tactical team, they would set up, gear up, and try to slow things down—freezing time and then deploying officers and tactics, maybe even negotiate. The problem at Columbine was the killing continued while police were doing this. Neither of the killers wanted to negotiate. It was a new level of lethality and police across the nation have been training ever since, not only for schools, but industry as well. Because, you see, the Boogeyman likes to take his hunting anywhere. Mandalay Bay Resort in Las Vegas, luckily, is an extreme example, but I would predict it will not be the last of its kind.

But before the police show up, you have to survive. You have to buy the time until the sheep dogs arrive.

Here is one thing you have to understand—time will move slowly because there are several steps that have to happen—each of which eats time—to get help to you.

First, someone has to call the police. This seems pretty basic, pretty simple. Usually, that is the manager or like in a school, the principal's secretary, the Dean or site security. If they are grouped in an administrative area like most businesses, it would not take long for an attacker to move through that area and annihilate those very people that have access to the lines of communication—outside lines, public address systems, and the like. This can quickly put a facility in to darkness, if the attackers know who to hit first—delaying the call for help. What that means is the initial contact with police via 911 is not a given **Don't assume someone has made that call. If you can, make it yourself.**

Look at your facility. Look at your surrounding areas. What could happen if the above scenario about the attacker destroying the outside communication was true?

Delay could be what leads many into a fatal action.

A quick and sometimes lucky response could be what saves us and others.

Ask yourself what you do when you hear a noise that does not sound 'normal.' I think many of us go looking for the source of that sound, to answer the question of what it actually is. We might not seek cover and initiate an action plan until we see the threat with our own eyes. That delay could be fatal—to everyone. A quick and sometimes lucky response could be what might save us and others.

Second, if a call gets to 911, it takes us to the next sequence of events and clear thinking needs to be employed because there needs to be understanding on the part of the 911 operator. He or she does not know what you know. Operators need to have things explained to them, clearly and calmly, so they can rally help. They need to find out as much as they can and will ask questions. Usually, the operator talking to you has a partner who is talking and dispatching units and working on getting resources to you, but all this takes minutes no one has to spare.

Third, after information is given, the operator will keep you on the phone. Keep the operator informed and answer their questions. They will ask you questions like 'what is happening now?' and, if they hear something, they may ask you to clarify what it is, but help is coming. Whisper, or don't talk at all, if you feel your voice will give up your location.

Getting small and getting quiet is the direction you want to go in unless you can run away. Putting distance between you and the threat is always good. Common sense says don't make noise, including talking—the attacker will hear you. Units have to travel to you and then find the threat. They are not coming to you, to free you. Get that out of your head now. Once you hear sirens don't think they will make their way to you directly. They may, if they can get you out before they neutralize the shooter, but plan on still being your own bastion of safety for a while. And about sirens, you may not hear them. Officers may arrive without sirens, not wanting to let the shooter know they are close and where they are.

They are going to the threat, to where the noise and killing is coming from. Once they stop that, they will come to you. Figure this:

> Common sense says don't make noise. Don't talk if the attacker might hear you.

- A phone call to 911 and giving them enough information to start units rolling to where you are—one to three minutes.
- Travel time for the first unit to arrive—4 minutes in a city, longer in the county.
- Finding and engaging the threat—4-10 minutes, depending on the size of the facility.

By my math, that is nine to seventeen minutes before the police can distract and engage the threat from the time they get the 911 call. It doesn't mean the threat is not still harming victims. It just means they are now having to deal with the police as well. Add more time for rescue and you will see you need to be on your own for a while—a very long while it will seem.

You and your colleagues need to get small and get quiet.

To be realistic, you might want to just double that number in the time estimate. I would plan on not seeing the good guys for at least 20 to 25 minutes, depending on so many variables.

There is another layer to this and we keep asking the question. What are you willing to do to live? Are you willing to fight? If so, fight with what? When we started this journey I told you about our Lockdown practice. I arm myself with a pen because that is what I am carrying always with me. Scissors would be good if I remember them, but it is not a routine. A pen is routine. If I thought about it before I moved from behind my desk I would probably get the scissors, the long sharp ones I have in the back of the center drawer of my desk.

What about the small American flag on a long wooden stick with the pointed fleur de lis at the mast head? That would give me some reach as they came through the door. Maybe you have had a need to use a cane because of a bad hip or knee. That could be used. Many people have pepper spray on their car key chain. That is a great weapon, but you need to practice with it. Blow back can wipe out both you and the shooter—or worse, wipe you out and do nothing to the shooter. Don't just think about the item, think how you would use it. Would you aim for the eyes or neck, or groin with that pen or flag? Yes to all.

> Don't just think about the item, think about how you would use it.

of them. And you do not do so passively, you do it with gusto and with all you have.

You will only have one shot and it needs to be a winning blow. If you are going to fight, you fight violently and cheat. Cheat a lot. There is no honor in how you fight. The loser is on the floor and the winner is alive. There, that is the honor.

The point is, we need to think through these events. We cannot think of them when they arrive, we need to have an idea of their depth and calling on us before they occur or we will lose the fight. Sure, this is not what you went into education for, or the job you have, but it's a reality and one you have to deal with. This also applies to anywhere you are—the mall, church, or even at home.

Yes, home.

Things to Remember:

- *If you think something is happening, call 911 yourself and don't wait for someone else.*
- *What can you fight with in your room or work space?*
- *Help is coming. Trust it.*
- *Remember, you will be treated like a suspect so don't be upset if the police point a gun at you and tell you to put your hands over your head.*

Mark Williams

Thought Point:

Go back to the question at the end of the last chapter. Would you change your answer now thinking about the tools you might use in case of the shooter gets in the room? Looking around the room, what might you use to defend yourself? Why or why not?

Forty-Seven Seconds

A significant emergency event can happen in any business space—at nearly any time

Photo by Jake Nebov, Courtesy of Unsplash

Mark Williams

Get Small, Get Quiet

Crawling under your furniture in your cubicle, or hiding behind some boxes in the warehouse, or trying to fit thirty employees in to a lab closet is just not something you learned in your years of working or college classes on being an employer—but it should be. What about a manager at a fast food restaurant and you have to hide the entire list of employees on duty, along with an elderly couple from Hoboken sitting in the booth in a closet corporate converted to an office.

It becomes a math issue: If the office is a rectangle or a square the formula is: $V = L \times W \times H$.

If you are in Nebraska and hiding in a grain silo its $V = \pi R2\ H$. There, that is the extent of objective application of placement of a solid or multiple solids, inside a void.

This only helps if you plan on piling people on top of each other. The question is, can you fit a volume of humans in a certain space so they become invisible for about fifteen to twenty minutes? Personnel, like employees or customers, when they get small and get quiet, need to take their 'luggage' with them, their backpacks, purses, lunch bags and the like. The office area, restaurant etc, needs to be clear, as if the entire room has left or has never been there—if there is time and the shooter hasn't already seen the area. This is in case those sight lines we talk about actually can be used by the shooter and he or she can see in to a room or work space.

You really need to make it look like the area is empty, so they keep moving away from you. This all depends if you have time. Time, that pesky item, is always against us. If time runs out, leave the luggage.

You might think, "Well, if we all did this, eventually they are going to think something is wrong and they will come back and take a closer look or force their way in."

It is common sense to think this way, but here is what you are doing: you are burning up time. Time they are taking to find someone to shoot is time law enforcement is using to get to you. Also, it is not too uncommon to be at a job, at least during lunch, whole buildings are empty because the schedule dictates lunches or meals or breaks happen at a certain time. Offices, especially small offices with less than a dozen employees, often shut down for an hour so everyone goes at the same time.

This is a small chapter but critical. During a lockdown or even a shelter in place—and with really no other events we are talking about, you want to disappear. Short of a Hollywood movie, you can't do that, of course. But you can become as insignificant, as small, as quiet, as possible, in order to cause some individuals, like those wanting to kill you, to think you are not there.

Like we had mentioned, when you look at the subjects who have been involved in assaulting business locations, synagogues, schools, many were on drugs. They could have been heavy pain narcotics, psychotropics, or some other substance. Much of it was prescribed. These individuals are wound up tight. They may be one trigger pull, one event, one conflict away from being set off.

> If we are talking about a room with students or even other individuals in it. You, as the supervisor or person in control of that space, need to think it through.

In the Bank of America shooting in North Hollywood in 1997, the two heavily armed suspects had several layers of body armor on the outside of their bodies, and several more layers of narcotics on the inside. Both had been shot several times and yet they kept going, expending almost 1200 rounds of ammunition and wounding thirteen of our na-

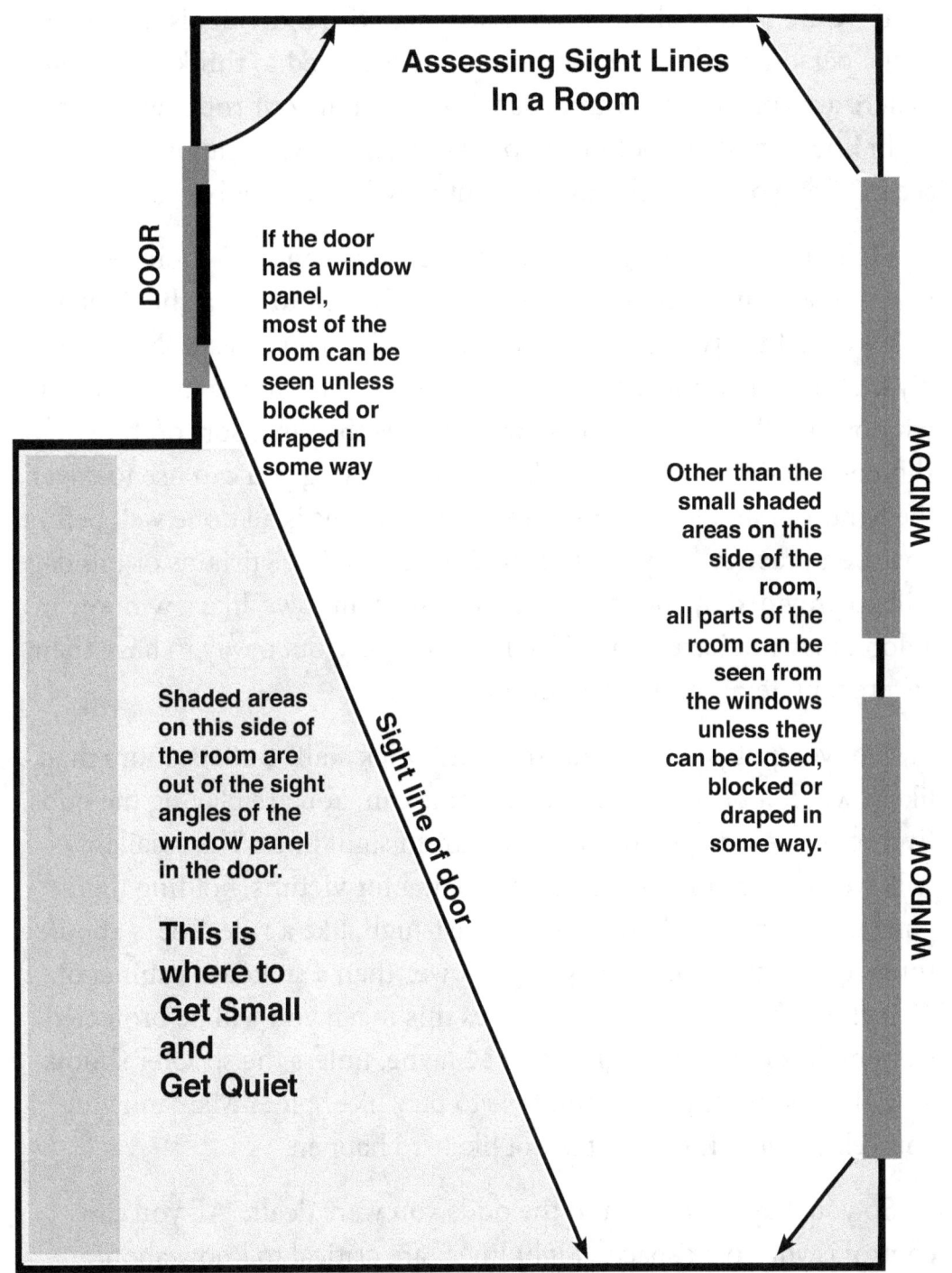

Where are you going to hide? Find out now, before trouble comes.

tion's finest police officers. It wasn't a school shooting, but it was in our collective neighborhoods, while we make a deposit or shop in the store down the block.

The rounds used can travel for a mile and half.

We could be shot and never hear the bullet that hit us.

If we are talking about a room or space with individuals in it, you, as the person maybe in control of that space, need to think it through. Where are you going to camp? Is there a wall in your room away from 'sight lines,' windows both interior and exterior, which allow people to see in? Can you cover them? Find out now, before trouble comes.

Sight lines are those lines of sight someone can see—their field of vision. Look out a window. Look to the left, then to the right. That arc of left to right is your sight line angle. It's what you can see. Now, apply that to your work space. Stand outside and try to see in through a window or other visual access point. This is the same sort of thing a shooter will do. Curtains, blinds, paper, anything you can use to cover the windows should be considered. Oh, and this is all done well before you even practice—if you practice. Much of it, like curtains or blinds, will be provided by the business, but some windows, like a window in a door, may not have either. You need to figure out a way to have them covered, preferably before an event.

Can you put yourself against a solid brick wall? Bullets, more than likely, will not penetrate brick, but some can. You are playing the odds. Everyone needs to get low and away from sight lines. The assailants will, we hope, be moving quickly, looking for victims, holding their guns either up like a hand gun or waist-high, like a rifle. That's about three feet off the ground. Try to get lower than a standard cabinet of 32 inches. The lower the better. Does this mean you will be protected from bullets flying through the air? Maybe, unless the shooter shoots low. Then your only opportunity is to play like Spider Man and glue yourself to the ceiling. That is not likely to happen.

So you play the cards and the odds you were dealt. All you can control is your own space. "Sight lines" are critical to know about.

> The assailants will, we hope, be ... holding their guns either up like a hand gun or waist-high, like a rifle. That's about three feet off the ground.
>
> Try to get lower than a standard cabinet of 32 inches.

In the case of the room above, the attacker can look through the glass pane in the door. If all your employees or customers and their belongings are hidden against the cabinet area, they are out of the shooter's sight line.

What he sees within his sight lines is an empty room.

Then again, if those blinds were down, he would see nothing at all. If he sees nothing, and the door is locked, he will likely move on.

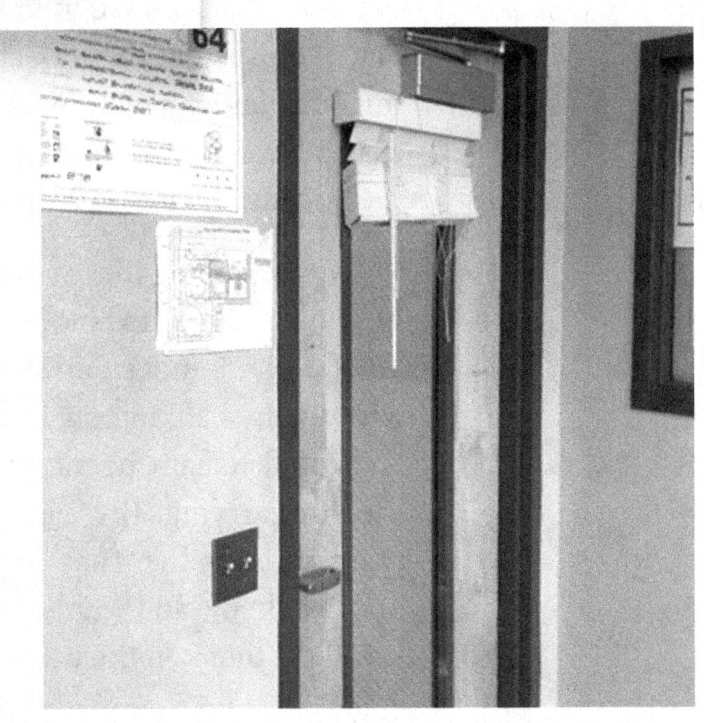

What can someone see in your room from the outside? Remember from prior chapters, these offenders may be hearing at a level we don't perceive. They very well could be hallucinating that they hear something from your room. You can't do anything about that. But don't give them a free shot.

Take away the sight angles as well as any other stimuli that would attract them to your room. Examine these stimuli for yourself. If, when you look in to your room, you cannot see anything to the right of the white board or map, or bulletin board, then that is where you can put your staff, on the floor, with all their belongings. Make the room look like you're off to a conference to Uruguay. If you are sheltering for weather, strong walls or doors offer you the best protection from a collapsing roof. Same space, but for a different reason.

Page 58 shows a drawing of what I mean by sightlines and how they might apply to any work space. Including yours. In the 'SAFE' areas, the angle of view is such anyone looking through the windows will not be able to see individuals in those locations marked SAFE.

If you have a space like this, you need to check that view for yourself. See if you can see in to the room and how much you can see, then place your people or yourself in that location. Sometimes, the best spot might be under a window. The graphic I give has two windows. Many spaces have none or just one. Two means you have a corner office to the outside. That is pretty rare, but prepare for that event.

We are hoping these violent people don't want to linger. They have maybe already tasted blood and want more. They will keep moving. Their body cannot stand still nor will they be patient. At least, that is what we are banking on. They also know the police are on their way and could actually be monitoring the police scanner with something they are carrying. There is a phone app that allows people to listen to police radio traffic. They could know the police are coming before you do. They know and want that to happen. They want the confrontation. It will get them on the news.

Placing your co-workers somewhere safe can be pretty challenging, especially when you have sliding glass doors or a wall made up of win-

> Something as simple as closing the blinds and locking the door might just be enough to keep anyone outside from trying to enter.

The best place for people to hide could be right under a window, either interior or exterior. That would depend on the sight lines, of course—looking left and right but also down.

dows, or windows on both sides of the room. Something as simple as closing the blinds and locking the door might just be enough to keep anyone outside from trying to enter. The wall, if there is one to the left or right of a glass door, actually might be the wall to put your staff against. If the shooter can see in, the idea is to have them see an empty room. The wall might be reinforced, meaning block, providing protection from bullets punching through the wall and in to the room.

Maybe you can hide under the very window you would otherwise be concerned about being seen through. If the windows are draped and the room is dark enough, the best place for staff could be right under a window, either interior or exterior. That would depend on the sight lines, of course—looking left and right but also down. The attackers will probably come from the hall door, however. They are probably already inside the building since that is where they want to be, and they want to come in from that side.

Again, focus on your space's sight lines. In these areas, we need to close the blinds, turn off the lights, cover the door window and lock it. The drawing shown earlier is just a general idea, but your work space may not be too different. What if it is a cubicle? Could you get small and get quiet under your work station and tucked behind the drawer or filing cabinet?

Many offices or work sites have interior and exterior windows. Some businesses might as well be doing work in a fish tank—doors with windows in them, walls of windows. That's great for light in the room, not so much for wanting to actually keep someone from seeing inside.

As mentioned earlier, the idea is to plant yourself and your staff members outside of that angle. If the attacker can't see you, they really don't know if anyone is present and there is a likelihood they will move on to an easier target. Remember, you're on your own for a while. No help should be expected. You need to prepare your space so it is absolutely still and quiet and with no indications that anyone is there.

You have seconds to prep it for a lockdown. Again, why was mine forty-seven seconds? It is how long it takes me to turn off my lights,

> You are already standing by a door or hunkering down behind your desk. How much more of a leap of rality is it to wonder what if someone actually comes through the door?

close the blinds, lock the doors, and stuff a class of 34 adolescents or co-workers in a space the shape of a slice of pie and only big enough for twenty of those students or workers—to get them down and quiet, making sure they are not on their cell phones texting.

It is a number established over years of training and execution, so, maybe it is scientific? It's my number, a number I know I can do, have done, to secure my classroom—my workspace to make it small and quiet. You need to establish your own number, and I challenge you to beat mine.

Bad guys on drugs can hear the change and car keys moving in your pocket. You want them to try the door, find it's locked and keep going down the hall. It's bad for your fellow staff members down the hall, but it's all you can do. That, and deciding what you're going to do when or if Evil comes through the door. Do you negotiate or do you fight like a momma badger on meth?

Earlier in this book, I told you I am standing by the door with a pen in my hand. I have rehearsed and actually practiced the movement I would make on an intruder. I have told that story to other staff members—educated individuals, whose response was, something along the lines

'Do you think we really need to?'

There can be a huge denial issue. Who wants to answer 'yes' to that scenario? You are already standing by a door or hunkering down behind your desk. How much more of a leap of reality is it to wonder what if someone actually comes through the door?

There is more than just getting small and getting quiet. Like Columbine, where students and faculty actually did get under desks and tables, there is a point where you might have to decide what are you willing to do to save your own life if they come in and start shooting those under those desks and tables. Are you willing to fight and with what?

Forty-Seven Seconds

Things to Remember:

- *Have windows covered, or able to be covered quickly, in your space.*
- *Look from outside your space as if you are an attacker, trying to see in. Find the site angles for each location you are looking from.*
- *Hiding places are outside the sight angles.*
- *If you have a reinforced wall or other protection, consider it as a hiding place or barricade location.*

Thought Point:

What can I use to cover windows quickly if there are no curtains or shades?

_____
_____
_____
_____
_____
_____
_____
_____
_____
_____

Mark Williams

Photo by Adolfo Felix, Courtesy of Unsplash

Forty-Seven Seconds

Weather Events

Barometer, n.:

*An ingenious instrument which indicates
what kind of weather we are having.*

—Ambrose Bierce (1842 – 1914)

I live in Phoenix, Arizona. In the summer time here, it gets stupid hot. When my son went to Iraq, he told me about his knee pads melting to the dashboard of the Humvee when they were on patrol. Maybe he wins the contest between us for most miserable place in the summer. But Arizona has communities where heat in those locations makes Phoenix look like a nice, cool oasis.

In Arizona, heat can kill you. In our northern and outlying areas, the cold can. In the summer, when the monsoons come in, we have hundreds of lightning strikes an hour—hundreds. You don't even have to be hit by lightning to be killed. Being near a strike can take you out.

This section is not about specific weather theory. This section asks you to consider how weather can threaten you, your employees, customers or work location—and to prepare. The biggest killer compared to all other weather issues is heatstroke, but that doesn't mean we ignore those weather issues.

In the Midwest, tornados plow through towns, in some regions, they can sneak up on you in the middle of the night. Imagine waking up to your house exploding because of the vacuum the tornado caused. Now, they have tornado sirens. The siren sounds when there IS a tornado. They don't mean there might be a tornado, there actually is one. If you hear one, what do you do? You may have only seconds to react, but it is much better than waking up to one in your living room taking Toto away. Recently, a man was interviewed sitting in what was left of his house. Actually, there was no house left. He said there was no siren, just that familiar sound of freight train associated with twisters. He grabbed his family and made it to the basement in time. When they came out, the house was gone.

What is your evacuation plan? Evacuation to a cellar is an escape plan. What if you were at work or out in the open?

In California, wild fires form their own weather system. In a tornado, in the middle of the country, most people have basements just for this. In California, a basement might cook you to death. Have a plan. Think about a weather system for your area and plan for it.

In winter, for example, many people in the east and northeast, pack blankets and water with snacks in their car just for moments like the ice storm this year on I-95 which caused thousands of motorists to ride out a couple of days in their car—on that highway.

Arizona, actually, is a moderate earthquake zone. Did we have a school plan for an earthquake? No. I can tell you we didn't, so one of the other events we have talked about would be adapted to fit— evacuation, Shelter in Place, reverse evacuation (coming in from the outside to the inside).

> This section asks you to consider how weather can threaten you, your employees, customers or work location...

What about flooding? As I write this, *a hurricane* just did a flyby of the east coast. Lots of rain and flooding will go on for days. Focus on what you have available as far as plans, evacuation routes. If there is none, what could you do as a staffer to minimize weather impact on your work space or business?

What if the lights go out, which means the air-conditioning probably went too, as well as the computer—there goes the electronic grid! But it also means your email connecting you to management is gone. Now what?

The rules to a lockdown or a Shelter in Place can serve you here. You need to survive until help arrives.

Survival might not include staying in your room, as you would in a lockdown. Survival might mean a basement or hallway—the kinds of spaces that are usually reinforced. It might mean evacuating to another shelter somewhere else. If you think it through in advance, you won't lose precious seconds wondering where the best place might be.

Flooding, rapid flooding where roads are quickly washed away, might mean you are staying at the office for a while because there is no open way to leave.

And let us never forget hypothermia. Even in the spring or fall, those months that hip to both ends of summer, if a person gets wet it could result in the body core getting to a dangerous level *(Brody, 2017)*. If the body core gets to 95 degrees from its regular 98.6, there is a good chance death can occur. Warming the body, getting the body out of the environment that is causing it to freeze, is the only way to save the person from freezing.

Hypothermia's cousin is heat stroke. A warning sign for this is red skin and no sweating and the person is usually unconscious. Evacuating to an unshaded environment in high heat can cause the body to overheat and eventually stop sweating. When that happens, body parts begin the process of dying as well.

In both cases, staff needs to think about where they are going and for how long. Don't wait for someone to tell you what to do, have a

plan for it yourself. One of the saddest stories ever to come out of the 9/11 plane strikes was some individuals were told to return to their cubicles and wait for the fire department to arrive and that someone would get back to them. No one did. Most of these were above the impact area and making it down quickly became impossible, but the idea of sitting and waiting, well.

I talked to an employee of a business in northern Minnesota once. We swapped stories about personal modifications to job space. I told him about my thirty feet of 400 pound test rope with the knots tied into it every foot or so in case we need to flee our second story room from a shooter.

He frowned at me.

He told me he had about fifty feet of rope in his cabinet, but that was in case one of the employees fell in the lake next to the school or through the ice that hadn't set up yet. He could throw it to them and they could be dragged out to safety. I frowned at him.

It's all perspective.

Forty-Seven Seconds

Things to Think About:

- *Does your job location have a plan for weather?*

- *Can you find safety quickly if you are outside?*

- *Do you have a communication plan or system to tell people where you are evacuating to, and to seek help from rescue resources or to inform administration personnel or others who need to know?*

- *What do you do and where do you go if a weather emergency hits when you're outside?*

- *Where do you go if you are inside and a major event is happening outside—such as a tornado or lightning storm?*

- *How does your business communicate with families of employees if needed?*

- *Do you have emergency supplies easily accessible, in case you need to stay there for hours? Ask your office if they have a weather evacuation or action plan. Keep it in a file that you can access.*

- *Rehearse your weather plan if it is significantly different from your shelter or lockdown plan.*

- *Hypothermia—plan on warm clothes.*

- *Heat stroke—plan on water needs.*

Thought Point:

Think about the most significant weather event in your area and when such events might happen. Do you have a plan? Write it down as:

'In case of_____I will do_____'

_____
_____
_____
_____
_____
_____
_____
_____
_____
_____
_____
_____
_____
_____
_____
_____

Forty-Seven Seconds

What Will I Do To Survive?

*The notion that the only alternatives to conflict
are fight or flight
is embedded in our culture,
and our educational institutions have done little to challenge it.
The traditional American military policy
raised it to the level of a law of nature.*

Richard Heckler—In Search of the Warrior Spirit

One decision that you need to think about, and I am not too sure you can overthink it, is: **what are you going to do to stay alive?**

Lt. Col. Dave Grossman has made a career out of traveling and teaching law enforcement and military personnel how to survive in life and death events. Grossman talks about different responses being common—***fight or flee*** being the most common. But within our own species, there is *posturing and submission.* The first two are very obvious: do we fight or run like we stole something when it comes to an active threat? But the next two are interesting as well (Grossman).

The posturing aspect is like playing poker. What cards do you have, and do you think your hand beats mine? Someone with a gun or a bomb usually always wins at this posturing level. At least for fifteen minutes. But what about submission?

In Arizona, in 2000, an elementary teacher faced a gunman in her elementary class with almost 30 young students. The teacher talked to the young teenager and, eventually, got him to release everyone as well as saving his own life by surrendering (Hostage, 2000). We could label this as a form of submission, giving the gunman the authority because he has the weapon and relinquishing our own authority to them, at least for a while. But what was appearing to be an act of submission was an act of posturing. Control went from the young man with the gun, to the teacher, without the student even knowing he was losing control.

Posturing gives the threat a feeling of being in charge, but this woman used that time, and the limited trust she built through what seemed to be submission, to begin an active dialog. One that paid off for everyone. The goal being to go home alive at the end of the day and in this case, everyone did, including the troubled youth.

At Columbine, there were no negotiations. If you made any noise, you were targeted. So, what are you going to do? The answer to this question can land you in waters you've never imagined finding yourself.

For example: You, as a staff member, are not required to sacrifice or even risk your life, to save your staff. It may surprise most of you to learn that police are not required to do so either. You would not be successfully sued in court based on that simple fact. However, most teachers and police would do whatever it would take to save the class, the school, everyone.

Grossman talks about 'emotional stamina.' He is predominantly talking about soldiers and law enforcement in high risk combat-type situations, but when you compare a fire fight in Laos to a gun fight in North Hollywood, San Bernardino, or Columbine, the only difference is the terrain and you aren't armed with the same weapon being used against you. You need to decide what you are willing to do to save your own life. If you have a plan for your life, the others in the room will also benefit. They will follow you. They will quickly figure out you are acting out of knowledge and the closer they stay to your hip pocket, the greater likelihood there is they will also live. You also have to remember the whole brain-shut-down-waiting-for-orders issue we talked about earlier. The people in the room with you will probably not have had the luxury training unless you, yourself, trained them. They will sit and wait while their brain tries to catch up with its analysis of what is happening.

Again, you need to get back to thinking things through. In places like the Charleston church shooting and Columbine, people actually pled for their lives. This could be a form of posturing or submission and might work, but think about what happened leading up to you pleading for your life? Did you just witness a series of people being shot by the individual you are pleading with? Did someone else just plead for his life and get shot anyway? How does that bode for you trying the same thing?

Who was it that said 'insanity is doing the same thing and expecting different results?' Time to think of alternatives?

Let me give you some examples from the school where I worked, and let you run with them. There are no experts in this—other than instructors in hand to hand combat. I think they would read this, knowing it is not addressed to other warriors, and maybe agree with some of the suggestions. Some of this comes from my personal experience as both a teacher and a former police instructor in non-lethal application. We used to call my class 'Close Quarter Crisis Management.' I liked the name, but if you have never been in a hand to hand altercation with someone, it is exactly that, management of yourself as well as your opponent bordering on escalation of fear.

Mark Williams

My room was on the second floor. There is only one way out of my room, the door, unless I consider the windows an escape. So, I went and purchased about thirty feet of 400 pound test rope, tied knots every two feet or so and have it rolled up in a box next to my desk. There! A poor man's elevator out the window to the ground floor. I've even walked through how to tie it off or hold it and allow students to descend, me being the last one out. I've already made that decision.

What if you are one hundred pounds soaking wet and don't have the girth to hold a rope, then what? Think through it. Can you tie it to a desk? Another form of anchor in the room? What if you jump? Can you jump? Broken legs can mend. Getting shot in the head can't.

If we are locked down, and I take a position by the door, what am I armed with? There are two people coming through that door, the good guys or the bad guys. I'm not worried about hurting the good guys in the uniforms. Based on my training and thought process, however, I am going to deliver as much violence to the bad guy in the shortest amount of time as I can. A pen can do that. So can a pencil. I have those. We're a school after all, we're suppose to. Scissors from my desk, anything sharp, delivered to the eyes, throat, or if I am lucky, directly up the nasal cavity. That road leads to the body's 'on/off' switch.

A while ago, a student ran on campus with a gun. It was a toy gun but we didn't know that at the time. We just saw, on the cameras, a young man carrying a chrome plated revolver. The school went in to a full lockdown and I was tasked with looking in rooms for a blond kid in a light blue shirt. I have a master key and started to open a teacher's door. It was blocked with a science table turned on end and I could see him, on the other side, holding up a baseball bat. Our eyes met and I could see him relax.

He had made his mind up as well.

If you have never thought about these situations, you might feel this 'education-based' discussion doesn't apply to you. Maybe you're at home or at your insurance office. It all still applies, believe me.

I was in a discussion with our school resource officer and a couple of staff members who are younger than myself—by decades.

> I am not worried about hurting the good guys in the uniforms.
>
> ... however I am going to deliver as much violence to the bad guy in the shortest amount of time as I can.

The discussion began by the first woman seeing his Taser on his belt and saying she wanted one for home protection. She was feeling like she needed something. She was young, pretty, small, and living alone.

We talked about guns, Tasers, and my favorite, pepper spray, or what, in the trade, is called OC spray for 'Olio-resin capsicum'. Basically, ground up pepper seeds in an aerosol spray that, when applied, gets in your eyes and nose and mouth and burns like eating your Grandma Edna's ravioli—on the sun. I was the training guinea pig for our agents and we video-taped it. That tape later became part of the training package for the State. If you want to see what happens when you spray someone with a 10% solution of that stuff, I suggest watching Williams have a snot bath for 45 minutes.

The second woman eventually cut in and asked why we were trying to talk her friend in to buying any of these things? Why 'promote violence' with these tools? Her implication was that nothing of the kind would ever happen.

She was a highly educated individual, talking as if this type of event was not going to happen and that absolutely anything can be handled with common-ground discussion and easy listening. The SRO and I eased our way out of the discussion, shaking our heads. We had just observed a victim with the opportunity not to be a victim and yet, somehow, believing it would not happen to her. I wanted to ask her about buying car or life insurance and applying the same theories but thought better of it.

Ask yourself this question-do you wear a seat belt? Why? Are you going to crash today? If you're wearing a seat belt, you must think you are? Right? Or, are you just prepared *in case* you crash?

'Knowledge is power,' Thomas Bacon said in 1597.

Knowing and being prepared does not generate fear, but strength. It means I know what I am going to do, how I am going to respond. Whatever gets me to the end of the day and to my family alive, is what I will use to get there.

How about you?

> You are already standing by a door or hunkering down behind your desk.
>
> How much more of a leap of reality is it to wonder what if someone actually comes through the door?

Things to Remember:

- *There is nothing wrong with trying to talk to the subject, just know it might not work and have another plan.*

- *Can you run? Can you physically run?*

- *What can you fight with?*

- *Are there other ways out of your work space? How?*

- *Knowledge is power. Fear evaporates in the presents of knowledge.*

Thought Point:

I thought again about the question asked earlier—the one about what I would do if a person with a gun comes in my room or work place, or if I heard shots before they entered. I've decided I am going to do:

_____

_____

_____

_____

_____

_____

_____

_____

Postscript

Volumes of books could be written on what we've touched on here in so many pages. Some might argue certain points, debate their validity, or even their need. If you're reading this, you are probably all grown up, maybe have a kid—or six grandchildren, have your first job or eighth. You might actually teach at a school or work in a business where these ideas or concepts are not a priority and only thought of in the collective environment because some state law says they have to. I hope it will never happen to you.

I hope all you did with this book, at the end of your need for it, was to level a wobbly patio table leg. I really do. But if one day, after reading and doing some of the work in these pages, something happens and its readings might have helped, let me know.

My website is www.fortysevensecondsusa.com. If you have an idea, or thought to make it better, let me know. Sheep dogs never stop training for the wolf—ever. Even old greying dogs. I'd like to think we are the wisest of our kind for, we have lived to see old age. That was by a combination of luck and common sense, a term you've heard in this book abundantly.

We can never really slow down, never really not think of issues that might arise. Just a handful of years ago, no one had heard of the Islamic State or ISS or Al Qaeda or home invasions. Now we have other groups like Antifa and any of an assortment of groups growing up inside our borders.

As I write these words, it is March fourth in Arizona. Seven months ago it was 115. Tomorrow, it is snowing just north of town, so the section on weather and hypothermia, yeah, that is on my mind.

No matter what, I hope this book causes you to love your family and friends so much you would actually want to hang out with them more in your life. I hope that desire causes you to ask hard questions that are right up there with talking to your sick spouse or sick child and about what kind of funeral they want. Hard things. But it is in the hard stuff we find answers, preparation, and strength. Fear comes from the unknown. Knowledge can give power over fear.

Enjoy—and peace to you.

Mark J. Williams

Forty-Seven Seconds

Any Business, USA

On the next page is a tear out sheet of the four major emergency events you might have to deal with. You can tear that sheet out of this book and post it somewhere so you can see it. You don't want to have to go find it, you want to look up and there it is, nice and visible.

Mark Williams

At-A-Glance Emergency Procedures

LOCKDOWN INSTRUCTIONS

Announcement:
"This is a lockdown"

Procedure:
- Quiet your colleagues
- Secure rooms or space
- Get out of sight
- Ignore alarms
- Arm yourself
- Await further instructions

SHELTER-IN-PLACE INSTRUCTIONS

Announcement:
"Shelter in place"

Procedure:
- Continue working
- Lock doors
- Prepare for upgrade to lockdown
- Await further instructions

WEATHER EVENTS

Announcement:
Various by location

Procedure:
- Be aware of outdoor surroundings
- At outside facilities, be aware of evacuation routes or areas of refuge
- Follow any announcements of instruction
- When outside, take sufficient hydration/thermal protection

EVACUATION

Announcement:
Fire Alarm Sounds

Procedure:
- Staff gather personal belongings
- Proceed with colleagues to designated site as posted or previously determined
- Await further instructions

References

Arizona, State of; Http://www.ade.az.gov/schooleffectiveness/health/schoolsafety/ plansresources.asp

Bourne Jr., Lyle, Yaroush, Rita; Stress and congition; A cognitive Phycological Condition; http://psych.colorado.edu/~lbourne/Stress-Cognition.pdf

Brody, Jane; Hypothermia; New York Times Health Guide, 6 April, 2017; http://www.nytimes. com/health/guides/injury/hypothermia/overview.html

Bronx apartment fire, https://en.wikipedia.org/wiki/2022_Bronx_apartment_fire

Grossman, Dave; On Killing; Back bay Books, 1995, Little Brown Company, NY NY.

Hostage Situation Ends at Arizona School: ABC News.com; 24 October, 2000; http://abcnews.go.com/US/story?id=95261&page=1

Ray, Chris; Prepared Christian, situational Awareness, 2012 march 13; http:// preparedchristian.net/situational-awareness/#.WGaET-V0zU74

RK Instruments; What is %LEL and %UEL, 2013, April 22; http://www.rkiinstruments.com/pdf/FAQ_LEL_UEL.pdf

Ronningen, Audrey; In the Mind of a Killer: the Psychology Behind School Shootings; The Bottom Line; 2012, November 14; https://thebottomline.

as.ucsb.edu/2012/11/in-the-mind-of-a-killer-the-psychology-behind-school-shootings

Troup, Des; How Many Times will you Crash Your Car?; 2011 July 27; Forbes magazine; Insurance.com; http://www.forbes.com/sites/moneybuilder/2011/07/27/how-many-times-will-you-crash-yourcar/#674888d850f9

School Safety; http://www.nfpa.org/public-education/by-topic/property-type-and-vehicles/school-fires

School shooters, 35 school shooters/related violence, CCHR, The mental Health watchdog; https://www.cchrint.org/school-shooters/

Side of effect of common psychiactric drugs; CCHR International 6616 Sunset Blvd. Los Angeles, California 90028

Simone Robers, Jana Kemp, American Institutes for Research, Jennifer L. Truman, Ph.D., Bureau of Justice Statistics, Thomas D. Snyder, National Center for Education Statistics

Staff, Mayo: Stress Relief from Laughter;

Stress Management; Mayo Clinic, 21 June, 2016; http://www.mayoclinic.org/healthy-lifestyle/stress-management/in-depth/stress-relief/art-20044456

The Economist; Danger of Death;

2014, September 1; http://www.economist.com/blogs/graphicdetail/2013/02/daily-chart-7?fsrc=scn/tw/te/dc/dangerofdeath

U.S.A, http://www.cchr.org/sites/default/files/The_Side_Effects_of_Common_Psychiatric_Drugs.pdf

USDOJ Indicators of School Crime and Safety, 2012; June 26, 2013 NCJ 241446

Williams, M;

Law Officer Magazine, 24 April 2017; http://lawofficer.com/tactics-weapons/the-Lockdown/

WTC Disaster Shows Value of Evacuation Drills;

National Research Center of Canada: 1 Aug, 2003; http://911research.wtc7.net/cache/wtc/analysis/nrccnrc_evacuationdrills.html

Forty-Seven Seconds

Mark Williams
is also the author of
the following works of fiction:

Emancipating Elias

Holy Ground

Looking for Indianola

Father's Day

Labrelotte Bay

Last Ship from Vladivostok

Distant Vision

The Good and Kind Man

... as well as the original *47 Seconds*,
focused on the needs of schools.

All are available through Amazon.

Forty-Seven Seconds

www.ingramcontent.com/pod-product-compliance
Lightning Source LLC
Chambersburg PA
CBHW060430220526

45465CB00008B/3079